Koivisto 92

Orthodoxy and Heresy

ORTHODOXY & HERESY

**A Biblical Guide
to Doctrinal Discernment**

Robert M. Bowman, Jr.

BAKER BOOK HOUSE
Grand Rapids, Michigan 49516

Copyright 1992 by
Baker Book House

Printed in the United States of America

Library of Congress Cataloging-in-Publication Data

Bowman, Robert M.
    Orthodoxy and heresy : a biblical guide to doctrinal discernment /
Robert M. Bowman, Jr.
      p. cm.
    Includes bibliographical references.
    ISBN 0-8010-1024-1
    1. Dogma. 2. Heresies, Christian. I. Title.
BT19.B68 1991
262'.8—dc20   91-45848
                                             CIP

Scripture quotations are from the New American Standard Bible.

for my parents,
Bob and Maggie Bowman

CONTENTS

PREFACE

For most Christians today, the challenge of learning how to discern orthodox from heretical doctrine has apparently not been faced. Either they treat doctrine as minimally important and so regard charges of "heresy" as rude and unloving, or they treat doctrine as all-important and so regard anyone who disagrees with them in the slightest as a heretic. In short, most believers seem to think either that there are almost no heretics or that almost everybody but their own little group is a heretic.

The cause of doctrinal discernment, then, is in serious jeopardy. Although anticult and discernment ministries are mushrooming everywhere, many of them operate on the basis of an excessively narrow understanding of orthodoxy. Consequently, such groups are charged deservedly with "heresy hunting" and discredit the practice of doctrinal discernment. At the other extreme—and often overreacting to such heresy hunters—are those within the Christian community who reject any warnings of heresy among professing Christians.

In this book I will attempt to set forth a balanced approach to the issue of doctrinal discernment. In Part One I will present a biblical case for the practice of discerning orthodox from heretical doctrines. In Part Two I will offer guidelines for doctrinal discernment.

In order to make this book as useful as possible, I will avoid making references to specific heretical or suborthodox groups, doctrines, and practices. This is so it may be read without conflict by persons in religious groups which discourage reading literature that criticizes their beliefs. I will also avoid referring in this book to specific individuals whose approaches to doctrinal discernment differ from mine. In most cases these are people whom I consider sincere Christians. In addition, I will avoid quoting and citing sources other than the Bible so that what I say can stand as much as possible on its own. A bibliography of recommended reading is provided at the end of the book.

Regarding biblical citations, in most cases I simply give the reference and expect the readers to look up the passage on their own. Where I have actually quoted from the Bible, citations are taken from the New American Standard Bible.

My own theological convictions are those of Protestant evangelicalism. Most of what I have to say in this book, however, is compatible with other Christian traditions as well.

This book is in large part the fruit of my years of collaborative study and dialogue with the research staff of the Christian Research Institute. CRI is an evangelical discernment ministry that was founded by the late Dr. Walter Martin and with which I have been associated for over seven years. About half of the material in this book first appeared in the *Christian Research Journal*, and was edited for that publication by Elliot Miller and Ron Rhodes. Elliot and I have spent many hours together discussing these issues, along with Ken Samples and Rich Poll of CRI. CRI is one of the few discernment ministries that seeks to operate on the basis of the principles set forth in this book.

My thinking on these matters has also been helped by Vern S. Poythress of Westminster Theological Seminary. The Dialog, a Christian philosophy club in Fullerton, with participants from Catholic, Protestant, and Eastern Orthodox churches, also stimulated my thinking, especially on the matter of the criteria of orthodoxy.

Finally, my thinking on these questions has continually been challenged by my parents, Bob and Maggie Bowman. They more than anyone else have taught me to listen to the views of others, to respect tradition but not deify it, and to remember that doctrine without love is empty. This book is dedicated to them.

PART ONE

The Case for Doctrinal Discernment

1

Is Doctrine Really Necessary?

The words *doctrine* and *doctrinal* have become pejorative terms for many—along with words like *dogma*. Even many evangelical Christians, who do affirm certain doctrines, pay little attention to doctrine beyond a certain minimum.

Of the many objections to Christian doctrine, five may be singled out as especially influential. Doctrine is often said to be (1) irrelevant, (2) impractical, (3) divisive, (4) unspiritual, and (5) unknowable. The importance of doctrine can best be shown by presenting positive answers to these charges.

The Relevance of Doctrine

In popular thought doctrine has to do with insignificant matters that are irrelevant to most people. Although doctrine can be trivialized, Christian doctrine is extremely relevant to all people. Christian doctrine (i.e., the teachings of Scripture) answers the fundamental questions of life—questions such as who God is, who we are, and why we

15

are here (Ps. 8:3–8; Heb. 11:6). How we answer these questions decisively shapes the way we live. To ignore them is to go through life blithely unaware of what is really important.

Doctrine is particularly important because a sound proclamation of the gospel of salvation depends on an accurate understanding of what that gospel is, what salvation is, and how salvation is received (Gal. 1:6–9; 1 Tim. 4:16). Nothing less than our eternal future depends on it. I do not mean to imply that we must all become theologians and experts on every fine point of doctrine to be saved. But the church as a whole must take great care that it faithfully proclaims the *true* gospel, and every Christian has a stake in the matter. I will have more to say on this point a little later.

It is true that some doctrinal issues are less important than others. One of the most crucial functions of Christian theology, and one of the most neglected, is to sort out the really important—the *essential*—from the less important and even the irrelevant (see Rom. 14).

Thus, handled properly, doctrine is very relevant to human life, and pursuit of sound doctrine should therefore be the concern of every person at least to some extent.

The Practicality of Doctrine

It is common in our day to assert that practice is more important than theory—that *orthopraxis* (doing right) is more important than *orthodoxy* (believing right). But this assertion is itself a theory—something people think and then say, and then try to put into practice. The fact is that what we *think* determines what we *do*. Thus, doctrine—as something we think—affects what we do, and so has practical significance.

It should be recognized, of course, that the practical effects of doctrine have limits. Doctrine does not always or solely determine our actions, since people often act on desires or concerns contrary to the doctrines they hold. For example, someone may believe as doctrine that lying is wrong, but selfish or prideful thoughts may take precedence over doctrinal convictions and lead the person to lie. The practicality of doctrine is found not in *determining* our practice, but in *informing* it—in giving us the knowledge with which, by God's grace, we can do the right thing.

The point is that we should regard *both* knowledge *and* practice as important. Ultimately, what is important is that a person truly live in obedient fellowship with God and experience his love; in that sense, *of course* practice is more important than doctrine. But God himself has made it clear that he uses doctrine to further that practical goal in our lives.

The practical importance of Christian doctrine, then, is great indeed. Doctrine enables us to develop a realistic view of the world and of ourselves, without which we are doomed to ineffectual living (Matt. 22:23–33; Rom. 12:3; 2 Tim. 4:3–4). Doctrine can protect us from believing falsehoods which upset people's faith or lead to destructive behavior (1 Tim. 4:1–6; 2 Tim. 2:18; Titus 1:11). Doctrine also prepares us to minister to others (Eph. 4:11–12).

The Unity of Doctrine

Perhaps the most common criticism people voice about doctrine is that it divides people. And indeed, doctrine—in the history of Christianity as in other religions—has often been allowed to divide people in reprehensible ways. But in a crucial sense doctrine is intended to unite people.

While it is true that doctrine inevitably divides people, this is not something that can be avoided. People *think* different things, and they *do* different things on the basis of their differing beliefs. What is undesirable, however, is that doctrine should divide people who ought to be together, or that divisions should be expressed in wrong ways. That is, doctrine should not divide faithful Christians from one another, preventing them from having fellowship together. Nor should doctrine lead people to hate or mistreat people who hold different doctrines than they do.

The Bible commands Christians to divide themselves from false teachers or heretics on the basis of doctrinal factors (Rom. 16:17; 2 John 9–11). In doing so, they are to *stand together in unity* against heresy (Eph. 4:12–13). Thus, taking a stand against heresy can promote genuine Christian unity.

As Christians mature together in their understanding of biblical doctrine, they become more united as their thinking becomes shaped more and more along the same lines (1 Cor. 1:10). Moreover, a balanced understanding of doctrine can help Christians divided by doctrinal differences to be reconciled as they learn which points are minor or unsound and which are not (1 Tim. 6:3–5; Titus 1:9–14). It turns out that shallow understanding of doctrine easily promotes disunity among Christians, while deepening understanding of doctrine tends to foster greater Christian unity.

The Spirituality of Doctrine

Although some people regard the pursuit of doctrinal accuracy as an unspiritual intellectualism, sound doctrine is actually very important to sound spirituality. Christian doctrine teaches us about God, his purposes and will for our lives, what we are like spiritually apart from God's grace, how God's grace changes us—in short, everything we need to know in order to pursue true spirituality (Rom. 6:17–18; 1 Tim. 1:5, 10; 2 Tim. 3:16–17). Doctrine provides external, objective controls for our inward, subjective experiences so that we may discern genuine spirituality from fraudulent, artificial, or even demonic spirituality (Col. 2:22–23; 1 John 4:1–3).

In pursuing an accurate understanding of Christian doctrine, we are fulfilling one aspect of God's greatest commandment—that we love God with all our *minds* (Matt. 22:37). This commandment surely implies that we should take great care and make every effort to conform our beliefs and convictions to the truth (see Rom. 12:2)—and this means doctrine.

Something should also be said here about the relationship between *doctrinal* discernment and *spiritual* discernment. In 1 Corinthians Paul speaks more than once about spiritual discernment. The spiritual person discerns all things, including the things of the Spirit of God, which can only be discerned spiritually (1 Cor. 2:14–15). The members of the congregation were to exercise discernment concerning the prophecies that were delivered in the church (1 Cor. 14:29). And some Christians are specially gifted to discern evil spirits from the Holy Spirit (1 Cor. 12:10). On the basis of these and other passages, some Christians have thought that discernment never has anything to do with the exercise of the intellect. In their view, one discerns between good and evil in doctrinal as well as practical matters simply by listening to the inner voice of the Holy Spirit.

By no means do I wish to disparage the work of the Holy Spirit in giving Christians discernment. Certainly all Christians must depend on the Holy Spirit to illuminate their minds that they may clearly see the difference between good and evil, truth and error. And many Christians who are ill-equipped to study doctrine in depth are remarkably discerning.

It would be a mistake, however, to pit spiritual discernment against doctrinal discernment. For one thing, the view that discernment is purely spiritual is itself a doctrine. Moreover, such a sharp separation of doctrine and spirituality assumes a dichotomy between the mind and the human spirit. Since this assumption is also a doctrine, the whole argument is self-defeating. There are also biblical reasons to reject a dichotomy of mind and spirit (which I will not elaborate here).

For another thing, the Bible also encourages Christians to use their knowledge of Christian doctrine in discerning truth from error and good from evil. The classic example of this is 1 John 4:1–3, where John commands us not to believe everyone claiming to be speaking by God's Spirit, but instead to apply a doctrinal test (belief in the full humanity of Jesus Christ) to those making such claims. Similarly, in 2 John 9 we are told to watch ourselves and not be deceived by anyone who "does not remain in the doctrine of Christ." In 1 Corinthians, Paul not only speaks of *spiritual* discernment but also presents *doctrinal* arguments in answer to the heretical belief that "there is no resurrection of the dead" (1 Cor. 15:12–19).

Rather than pitting spiritual and doctrinal discernment against one another, we should see them as two sides or aspects of the same activity. True spirituality includes a submission of the mind to the teachings of the Bible, and sound doctrine includes the belief that our knowledge of the truth is dependent on the illumination of the Holy Spirit. Thus in true discernment at its best, the Christian operates holistically—drawing upon a God-given knowledge of biblical doctrine in sensitivity to the Holy Spirit.

The Knowability of Doctrine

Some people avoid studying Christian doctrine because they are convinced it is too difficult or complex to grasp. While small children, the mentally retarded, and certain others may be admitted incapable of understanding doctrinal matters, the vast majority of adults—young and old—are able to understand much more than they have bothered to learn. Every individual is responsible to acquire doctrinal knowledge as his or her mental faculties, educational level, and opportunities allow.

Scripture commands all Christians to learn doctrine. Generally, removable spiritual impediments—not irremovable intellectual ones—prevent Christians from advancing in doctrinal understanding (Heb. 5:11-14). Christ has given teachers to the church to assist believers in learning doctrine (Eph. 4:11). Obviously such teachers must master doctrine on a level beyond most other Christians, but they do so for the purpose of imparting as much truth as possible to the rest of the members of the body of Christ.

Some aspects of Christian doctrine, admittedly, are difficult and complex, and even highly trained theologians wrestle with them. But that shouldn't discourage us from studying Christian doctrine. That would be like a nine-year-old excusing herself from learning times-tables because there are some mathematical problems that puzzle even professional mathematicians.

Sound doctrine is difficult enough to require honesty and discipline, yet easy enough that—with the exceptions mentioned previously—all who seek God's grace and commit themselves to the task can learn it (2 Pet. 3:16-18).

Doctrine and Salvation

n discussing the relevance of doctrine, I mentioned in the previous chapter that a person's salvation can depend to some extent on doctrinal belief. Since this point is so often contested in our day, it deserves closer attention.

Almost everybody who acknowledges Jesus Christ in some way will agree that those who completely and explicitly reject Jesus Christ are lost. Many people find it difficult, however, to believe that some people might sincerely think themselves to be following Jesus Christ and yet, due to heretical belief, be lost. Jesus himself promised, "Seek, and you shall find" (Matt. 7:7); should not those who seek for Christ find him? And do not many sincere members of groups which evangelicals label heretical truly want to find Christ? They may read the Bible more studiously than many an evangelical church member; they may express an ardent desire to know God and obey him; they may zealously proclaim the message of Christ as they have been taught it. Are they not, therefore, seeking Christ, and will they not, then, in accordance with his promise, find Christ? And if so, how can salvation depend on doctrinal beliefs?

These questions may be answered by keeping the following biblical principles in mind.

(1) *Not everyone who acknowledges Jesus as Lord will be saved.* This follows directly from Jesus' own words in Matthew 7:21. Simply acknowledging that Jesus is Lord does not guarantee a person's salvation. The acknowledgment might be mere lip service, as demonstrated by refusal to obey him as Lord (Luke 6:46). Or someone might call Jesus "Lord" and not mean the same thing as what the Bible means by it. This leads me to a second principle.

(2) *Many who claim to acknowledge Jesus actually believe in "another Jesus," and are either deceived or deceiving.* This follows directly from 2 Corinthians 11:4. Many who speak of faith in "Jesus" have an understanding of who and what Jesus is that differs so much from reality that in truth they do not have faith in the real Jesus at all. If a person thought Buddha was another name for Moses, we would not normally consider him a Buddhist, no matter how piously and moralistically he lived out his belief in "Buddha." Similarly, someone who denies the biblical view of Christ should not be identified as a Christian, no matter how religiously he follows his belief.

Some people who believe in "another Jesus" are no doubt insincere, and Paul warns of "deceitful workers, disguising themselves as apostles of Christ" (2 Cor. 11:13). I like to think the best of people, even people with whom I have serious disagreements. But I have become acquainted with a few persons about whom I have had to conclude, reluctantly, that they are simply liars. These people know on a conscious level that the message they proclaim is false.

On the other hand, some people, even members of Christian churches, can be "led astray" (2 Cor. 11:3b) by such deceivers. Thus, it is possible for sincere people, even people who were part of the fellowship of true Christians, to be deceived into following "another Jesus."

Not that such people are perfectly innocent—rather, they are like Eve who, although deceived by the serpent (2 Cor. 11:3a), was guilty of sin and held accountable by God (Gen. 3:1–6, 13–16).

(3) *Those who are zealous in religious matters are not necessarily saved.* In Romans 10:2 Paul says of his Jewish brethren who rejected Jesus, "They have a zeal for God, but not in accordance with knowledge." Zeal, of course, implies sincerity—that is, the mental state of believing that what one is promoting is based on truth. The Jews who rejected Jesus were for the most part zealous, and therefore sincere in this sense—but they were still lost (Rom. 9:1–3; 10:1). Their zeal was, in particular, for a right standing with God—but they sought it on the basis of their own works, as if salvation was by works, rather than receiving the righteousness which was available in Christ through faith (Rom. 9:30–10:4).

Matthew 23:15 addresses zeal of another kind—zeal in seeking converts. The Pharisees were extremely zealous in missionary work, but all they succeeded in doing was leading more people into their error. Zeal in witnessing or evangelizing does not indicate that a religious group is God's people.

(4) *No human being truly seeks for God unless God's Spirit draws that person; therefore, those who appear to seek for God but do not come in God's way are not seeking for God at all.* In Romans 3:11 Paul quotes Psalm 14:2 to the effect that "there is none who seeks for God." Sin has so perverted the desires of all human beings that none of us, by our own natural wishes, is looking for God. This is because "the mind set on the flesh is hostile toward God" (Rom. 8:7). Of course, some people do seek for God, otherwise God would not call upon us to seek him (Isa. 55:6, etc.). But when people seek God, it is only because God has first "sought" them and drawn them toward him by his grace (Luke 19:10; John 6:44; 15:16).

When people therefore appear to be "seeking God"— when they study the Bible (2 Pet. 3:16), attend meetings, pray, change their life-styles, attempt to obey the commandments, even speak of their love for God and Christ—yet persist in worshiping a false God, or honoring a false Christ, or following a false gospel (2 Cor. 11:4; Gal. 1:7–9), we must conclude that they were not really seeking *God*. Rather, they may have been seeking spiritual power, or security, or peace of mind, or warm relationships, or knowledge, or excitement, or anything other than simply God. And in saying this, I am not claiming that all genuine Christians on the other hand have sought purely and simply after God. No, our testimony as Christians must be that we were also following our own divergent path when God sought us, stopped us in our way, and led us up a new and narrow path leading to salvation in Jesus Christ (Matt. 7:13).

(5) *Anyone who truly desires above all else to know the truth about God and his way of salvation can and will be saved.* This is the other side of the coin from the previous point. Jesus promised that "the one who comes to Me I will certainly not cast out" (John 6:37). However, we must come to the *true* Jesus on *his* terms. Judas came to the true Jesus, at least outwardly (actually, Judas did not know who Jesus really was), but he did not come on Jesus' terms and was consequently lost (John 17:12). The cost of abandoning heresy is usually great—the loss of friends, the embarrassment of admitting error, the threat of the heretical teachers that all who leave their teaching will be lost. But salvation is available for anyone who by God's grace puts truth (and the One who is truth) above these things.

3

Judging Others—
Is It Always Wrong?

octrine, as we have seen, is a necessary aspect of the Christian life, and we need to discern between truth and error in doctrine. Yet it might be suggested that while we need to discern such matters *for ourselves*, we have no right to presume to discern such matters *for others*. Who are we to tell others what to believe? Who are we to tell others that their doctrines are false? Should we not simply say, "I personally don't believe that, but of course you may believe whatever you wish"?

The answers to these questions are not as obvious as is sometimes thought. There are senses in which we are not to judge others, but there are also senses in which we must exercise judgment with respect to others. Sorting these out is crucial to doctrinal discernment.

When Judging Is Wrong

When is it wrong to judge others? Or, to put it another way, what sorts of judgments of others are wrong?

(1) *Hypocritical judgments.* No one appreciates it when people harshly criticize or condemn others for doing things that they are also guilty of doing. What makes this sort of criticism unacceptable is not merely that the person making the accusation is also guilty. Rather, what makes it offensive is that the hypocrite claims or pretends to be guiltless. The hypocrite pretends to be righteous when actually he is not. On the other hand, when someone says, "You and I are both guilty of this, and we need to do better," that is not hypocritical.

To put it another way, hypocritical judgments are not bad because they are *false* (they may or may not be). They are bad only in that they are spoken hypocritically. Hypocrites who judge others will have to face judgment themselves, and ought to deal with their own sins first (Matt. 7:1–5). But that does not disprove that what they say is true.

In fact, Jesus observed that the hypocritical Pharisees were typically right in what they said; their problem was that they did not follow their own good advice (Matt. 23:1–3). There is an important lesson for us here. If we are the recipients of a judgment that we feel is expressed by hypocrites, we should not dismiss it out of hand on that basis. Instead, we should consider if they might be right about us after all. God sometimes uses people to communicate truth to others even though their own motives are bad (Phil. 1:15–18).

Sometimes people try to dismiss all judgments by other human beings on the premise that none of us is perfect. That is so, of course; but that does not prevent us from sometimes being right in what we say. The warnings in the Bible against hypocrisy are not intended to paralyze us from expressing disagreements with others, but to draw attention to the primary importance of dealing with our own sin.

Interestingly enough, people who reject *all* judgments by other people fall unavoidably into a judgment of others themselves. That is, if I say, "You are wrong to judge others," I have just judged you myself. To avoid this dilemma, I might soften my position to something like, "I personally would never judge others," or, "I wish you would not judge others." If I do this, though, then I really no longer have any basis for complaint if others express judgment. The fact is that we all do regard some things that others do or believe as wrong, and nearly all of us express these criticisms verbally.

(2) *Unjust judgments.* Jesus said, "Do not judge according to appearance, but judge with righteous judgment" (John 7:24). Once again, it is evident here that Jesus is not forbidding all judging of others. It is *how* we judge, not *whether* we judge, that is the issue.

What sort of judgment is Jesus forbidding here? It is the practice of judging "according to appearance." Jesus does not mean here that we are to judge by ignoring the external evidence and reaching some mystical intuition. Nor does he mean that we are to make our judgments by trying to discern what is in a person's heart. The contrast is between not external facts and internal intuitions but mere appearance and true reality. In short, Jesus is warning against *superficial* judgment. Superficial judgments are those which look only at the surface of things and do not penetrate to the reality. Such judgments, of course, tend to be unjust.

Whereas hypocritical judgments may or may not be true, unjust judgments are always and necessarily false. They are based on a misinterpretation of the appearances, and thus fail to judge things as they really are.

How do we avoid misinterpreting appearances? That question is getting a little ahead of ourselves. But it is important to realize that it can be done. We can all think of examples in which someone misinterpreted what we said, only to realize later their mistake (say, after we pointed it out). Since this sort of correction happens all the time, it is possible for us to exercise just judgment.

(3) *Presumptuous judgments.* There are some matters on which human beings simply are not competent to

judge. We are not competent to rule on the question of whether some individual will be saved. Judgment, in this sense, is the sole province of Jesus Christ, the Son of God (John 5:22–23; Acts 17:31). Assuming the right to judge in this area is presumptuous. The power of salvation and destruction is not ours; therefore, we may not set ourselves up as eternal lawgivers and judges over others (James 4:11–12; 5:9).

Another sort of presumptuous judgment is taking nonessential matters and making them "litmus tests" for Christian fellowship. Paul explicitly warns against doing this with reference to matters of observances and dietary restrictions (Rom. 14:1–23). It would be presumptuous of me to assume that all Christians must agree with me on everything.

As before, it is clear that not all judgments are presumptuous. Therefore, the very real abuse of presumption should not be made the excuse for rejecting all judgments.

When Judging Is Right

What has been said already gives some indication of the kinds of judgments that are good and proper. Judgments that avoid hypocrisy, superficiality, and presumptuousness are going to be sound, valid judgments.

(1) *Judging truth from error and good from evil.* The New Testament is emphatically clear that we are to judge truth from error and good from evil. We are to do this, not merely as individuals, but corporately, as the church (Rom. 12:2, 9; 1 Cor. 12:10; 14:29; 1 Thess. 5:19–22). These passages especially focus on the need to discern true revelations from false revelations. Those who claim to be prophets, who claim to speak under the inspiration of the Spirit, must have their teachings tested by the teaching of the apostles and prophets in Scripture (Acts 17:11; 2 Pet. 2:1; 3:2; 1 John 4:1–2; Jude 17).

(2) *Judging unrepentant sinners in the church.* Both Jesus and Paul taught that those who commit serious sins that violate the integrity of the church, and who refuse to repent, should be excluded from Christian fellowship (Matt. 18:15–18; 1 Cor. 5:9–13). This is not a matter of judging their eternal future. It is not a matter of consigning them to eternal punishment. Rather, it is a matter of bringing discipline to the unrepentant and maintaining the integrity of the church. In other words, it is for the good of both the sinner and the church.

Again, note that this is the responsibility of the church as a whole, not of isolated individuals. Note also that Jesus indicates that the judgment must be made through due process. Such due process safeguards against superficial judgments.

(3) *Judging teachers of false versions of Christianity.* Not only are we obligated to reject for ourselves false prophetic revelations and false doctrines, but we are obligated to reject those who bring them. Once again, the Bible is explicit on this point (Rom. 16:17; Gal. 1:6–9; 2 Tim. 3:16–4:4; Titus 3:10–11). False teachers are to be identified, by name if necessary (2 Tim. 2:17), and the church warned not to support their teaching.

Again, our fallibility in making such judgments must be admitted, but it does not relieve us of our responsibility. If I saw some people about to drink acid in the mistaken belief that they were drinking water, I would warn them. I would not let the fact that I might possibly be mistaken prevent me from issuing the warning. If they disputed my claim, I would not let the matter drop, but would insist that they examine the fluid with me to make sure. Nor would I let the fact that I am not a chemist stop me from issuing the warning. Even nonchemists can tell the difference between water and acid, if they take the time to learn some basic facts about both.

Similarly, it is entirely appropriate to warn others that the religion they are "consuming" is bad for their spiritual health. Before we can do that, of course, we need to learn to tell the difference between true Christianity and false versions of the Christian faith.

Moreover, it is quite appropriate for some Christians to devote their attention to making such judgments and passing on their findings to the rest of the church. Just as we need consumer advocates to warn us about dangerous or defective or overpriced products on the market, we need people who can warn us about false or oversensationalized claims made for various doctrines circulating today. If these specialists do their jobs right, they teach us to take responsibility ourselves for avoiding the bad and making the most of the good. In doctrine, while some of us may be more gifted at discernment than others, all of us are called to exercise discernment.

Dodging Doctrinal Discernment

he practice of doctrinal discernment is strongly discouraged in some professing Christian circles today. There are some people who are critical of anyone who applies doctrinal tests to what others believe. The reason, in most cases, is simple: their doctrine cannot withstand the scrutiny of comparison with the doctrine of the Bible.

We might expect that religious groups that believe thoroughly heretical doctrine and claim to be the only true Christians would discourage people from developing the ability to discern good doctrine from bad. What is disturbing is to find that many people in certain circles within the community of orthodox, evangelical Christians also denounce the exercise of discernment. In this chapter we will consider some of the most popular arguments used to dodge doctrinal criticism.

"Don't Divide the Body of Christ"

Whenever the teachings of a professing Christian teacher or leader are questioned or criticized, you can be sure that someone will complain that such criticism divides the body of Christ. The critic is invariably accused of "sowing discord among the brethren" (a phrase based on Prov. 6:19), of being contentious or divisive, of creating dissension. And sometimes, they are right.

The fact is that in some cases those who are criticizing the teachings of others are simply being contentious. Sometimes people cause havoc and chaos by exaggerating doctrinal differences out of proportion. Divisiveness is a sin, one against which all of us involved in doctrinal discernment need to guard ourselves diligently.

That having been said, not all division is wrong. I have already explained in chapter 1 that Christians need to divide themselves religiously from non-Christians. That is the first point. If a group of people arises within the Christian church that begins to teach false doctrine so contrary to Christian beliefs that those following it can hardly be considered practicing Christians, the church has the *responsibility* (not merely the *right*) to divide itself from that group.

In fact, even if the people believing the false doctrine might be Christians, if the error is bad enough the church must take a stand for doctrinal truth that excludes the error and those who insist on teaching it.

In Romans 16:17 Paul writes, "Now I urge you, brethren, keep your eye on those who cause dissensions and hindrances *contrary to the teaching which you learned*, and stay away from them." Who is it, according to Paul, that causes dissensions? Is it those who teach different, false doctrines, or those who point out those who teach false doctrines? Obviously, it is those who teach the false doctrine. Those who "blow the whistle" on false teachers in the church are *not* causing the division.

Let's look at it another way. Suppose that in a particular church you have two groups of people. The first group adheres to the same doctrines the church has taught for decades ever since it was founded. The second group follows different doctrines that were introduced by a new teacher. These two sets of doctrines are radically different—so much so that we may be justified in saying that they embody two different and incompatible ideas of what it means to be a Christian. In that case, what do we have? We already have a division in the church. It is unavoidable. The two groups cannot possibly work harmoniously together. If their doctrinal beliefs are different enough, they will have two incompatible notions of what is involved in prayer, so that they can't even pray together.

Now, in such a situation, there is no harm in pointing out and admitting what is already the fact. It is not causing division to admit that division exists. Nor is there anything wrong with one group insisting that their doctrine is true and the other group's is false. After all, they both can't be right.

We need to make sure that we don't divide over nonessentials. On the other hand, unity at any price will not work. The "unity of the faith" must be maintained in accordance with a sound knowledge of Christian doctrine (Eph. 4:13–16). Too often those teachers who bemoan the dividing of the body of Christ have already divided it themselves by teaching false doctrine.

"Don't Touch God's Anointed"

When Christians voice concerns about the doctrines being taught by professing Christian preachers, you often hear the protest, "Don't touch God's anointed." Twice in the Bible we read of God saying, "Do not touch My anointed ones, and do My prophets no harm" (1 Chron. 16:22; Ps. 105:15). As this is used by some teachers today, this means that no one except God has the right to judge or even to criticize publicly the teachings of certain special teachers, who are regarded as God's "anointed."

What shall we make of this claim? Well, the place to begin is with the passages themselves. In context, the "anointed" individuals are almost certainly the patriarchs—Abraham, Isaac, and Jacob (1 Chron. 16:15–21; Ps. 105:6–14). Why they are called God's "anointed ones" is not certain. It seems that the term "anointed ones" is roughly synonymous with "prophets" in the second line. Although this usage is rare in the Bible, it can be found (1 Kings 19:16b; Isa. 61:1). It also fits the context, since the emphasis in the passage is on the unique role the patriarchs played as the ones through whom the word of God, the covenant, came to form the people of Israel.

On the other hand, it is evident that the patriarchs were *more* than prophets. They were men who were promised that their descendants would include kings that would rule over the land of Canaan (Ps. 105:11; Gen. 17:6, 16; 35:11). This is consistent with the fact that when the Old Testament speaks of God's "anointed ones," it almost always is referring to kings (e.g., 1 Sam. 2:10, 35; 2 Sam. 1:14, 16; Ps. 2:2; 89:38, 51; Dan. 9:25, 26; cf. 1 Sam. 16:12, 13; 1 Chron. 11:3; 14:8; 29:22; Isa. 45:1).

In any case, the "anointed ones" whom God said not to "touch" were not just teachers, preachers, evangelists, or religious leaders. They were unique figures in Israel's history invested with prophetic and royal authority and significance.

Now, indeed some teachers today also claim to be prophets, special spokespersons through whom God speaks today. But some people quote "Don't touch My anointed ones" and carelessly apply it to anyone whom they feel is a spiritually gifted teacher or minister. Such an application is clearly contrary to the meaning of the text.

Another point that needs to be made here is that what God forbade was for pagan kings to kill or otherwise harm God's "anointed ones." God did not forbid people to criticize his anointed ones. For example, in Genesis 20:7 God warned Abimelech, the king of Gerar, to restore Sarah to Abraham, "for he is a prophet." But this did not prevent Abimelech from questioning Abraham's deception (vv. 9–10). It is one thing to do violence against God's anointed; it is another thing to criticize them when they err. Even true prophets, when they are not speaking prophetically, can be mistaken (e.g., 2 Sam. 7:3, cf. vv. 4–17).

While it is true that we should not reject God's prophets, that still leaves us with the responsibility to determine who God's prophets really are. Not everybody who claims today to be a prophet of God can really be one, since they frequently contradict one another. If someone claims to be God's prophet but teaches false doctrine or proclaims false prophecies, we have every right to reject them—in fact, we must reject them (Deut. 13:1–5; 18:20–22).

In the New Testament, *the* Anointed One is Jesus Christ, who is prophet, priest, and king *par excellence.* All those who are united to Christ through his Spirit are in a sense "anointed" (2 Cor. 1:21). As such, we do not need "anointed" teachers with secret revelations of knowledge claiming special authority and telling us to trust them (1 John 2:20, 27).

The bottom line is this: The New Testament tells us explicitly to censure false teachers in the church (Rom. 16:17; 1 Tim. 1:3; Titus 1:11; 3:10–11). Therefore, no one has the right to hide behind the claim to be "God's anointed." If someone is teaching false doctrine, that is proof positive that they are in no sense God's anointed.

"Check the Fruit"

Whether someone is a true or a false teacher must be determined on the basis of that person's teaching. As obvious as that might sound, some people disagree. Some professing Christians today argue that teachers and ministers should be evaluated on the basis of the "fruit" of their ministry, not on the basis of a comparison between their doctrine and the doctrine of the Bible.

First of all—and by now this is a familiar point—the claim that doctrine should be evaluated solely by its fruit is itself a doctrine. We must first decide if this doctrine is true before we can have any confidence in applying it to other doctrines and those who teach them.

The biblical basis for this teaching is well known. Jesus himself said that we would know false prophets "by their fruits . . . A good tree cannot bear bad fruit, nor can a bad tree produce good fruit . . . So then, you will know them by their fruits" (Matt. 7:15–20).

As with the previous two objections to doctrinal discernment, this one has much to commend it biblically. Obviously, if Jesus himself said that we can tell false prophets by their fruits, that is a valid test.

The problem is that some people are using this passage as an excuse to avoid the scrutiny of their doctrine. There are, after all, other passages in the Bible that instruct Christians to apply *doctrinal* tests to professed Christian teachers (e.g., 1 John 4:1–2). So Jesus cannot mean that doctrine itself can never be the basis for testing someone's claim to be a prophet. Rather, it seems best to understand him to mean that examining the fruits of a person's ministry is *one* good way to test its validity.

One of the bad fruits of false doctrine is that it divides Christians. Again, this is not the fault of those who criticize the false doctrine—it is the fault of those who teach it. It is strange reasoning indeed to blame the division on those who object to the introduction of false doctrine!

Some of the claims to "good fruit" made by groups following bad doctrine must themselves be subject to discernment. For example, most if not all religious groups claim that its followers experience increased love, happiness, and self-fulfillment. The difficulty here is that these claims are largely subjective. No doubt for many unhappy people any sort of structured community of people committed to a common cause would provide such an experience. Please understand that I am *not* denying that true Christianity offers something unique in this regard. My point is that love, happiness, and self-fulfillment can be experienced by non-Christians on a natural, human level, and this experience should not be confused with the eternal benefits of knowing the true Jesus Christ.

Similarly, some groups that believe false doctrine claim that their beliefs must be true because they have experienced miracles in their midst—especially healings. Unfortunately, the Bible is quite explicit in warning us that false religious leaders will in some cases be able to produce false signs and wonders (Matt. 24:24; 2 Thess. 2:9). The Old Testament warned that God would sometimes allow a false prophet to perform a sign or wonder in order to see whether the people were more interested in impressive miracles than in the true God (Deut. 13:1–5). Therefore, we cannot assume that miracles are proof that someone's teaching is from God.

In saying that false teachers can produce some apparent miracles, I am not claiming that all miracle reports connected to false doctrine must be from the devil. We may not always be able to tell whether they are genuinely supernatural occurrences—in which case they must be ascribed to demonic powers—or not. False miracles might be tricks performed by charlatans, or they might be actual healings produced by psychosomatic causes. Then there is the possibility that God might heal somebody who listened to false doctrine but who did not understand its significance and whose faith was in the true God and his power. It is not terribly important that we always be able to make such judgments. What is important is that we not make the mistake of thinking that the occurrence of apparent miracles puts a divine endorsement on everything taught by the religious leader involved.

"Don't Name Names"

In some circles Christian leaders are willing to allow criticism of certain doctrines as long as the teachers of those doctrines are not identified. The idea here is that disagreeing with a doctrine is not divisive, but naming an individual and identifying him or her as a false teacher is divisive.

This argument assumes that it is wrong to "divide" the church over doctrinal matters. If a teaching is bad enough for it to be rejected by the church, then it is bad enough that those who insist on continuing to teach it must be identified and exposed.

The example of the apostle Paul is instructive. In some cases he chose not to mention the names of the false teachers (e.g., 1 Tim. 1:3). In other cases, however, he gives their names. For example, in one letter he mentioned Hymenaeus and Alexander (1 Tim. 1:20) and in another letter he mentioned Hymenaeus again along with Philetus (2 Tim. 2:17). Apparently, there is nothing wrong with naming false teachers.

One reason why giving names can be important is that if false doctrines are spoken of in generalities, people will often deny that their teachers are responsible for those doctrines. In many cases people will not believe that their favorite teachers are espousing false doctrine unless exact quotes are produced from their writings or sermons documenting the errors.

If someone is an unrepentant false teacher, we need to do more than reject that person's specific false doctrines. We need to have nothing to do with that person. "Reject a factious man after a first and second warning, knowing that such a man is perverted and is sinning, being self-condemned" (Titus 3:10–11). These are strong words, even harsh, but they are also inspired words from God. The person who creates factions by teaching different, false doctrine is to be rejected. For that rejection to be consistent throughout the church, the false teacher needs to be publicly named.

"Not Everyone Is a Theologian"

Some people, confronted with criticisms of certain teachers in the church, dismiss those criticisms by saying that the teachers in question don't claim to be theologians. The critics, they suggest, are imposing a standard on the teachers that is unfair. After all, we may be told, these individuals have as their primary calling not the teaching of theology or doctrine, but some other ministry. Perhaps they are evangelists or pastors; perhaps their claim to fame is their ability to motivate people, or their success in leading people to Christ, or the reports of healings taking place through their ministry. They may be unsophisticated, dynamic personalities who did not have the benefit of formal theological education but who feel a special calling to ministry. These teachers' ministries, it is concluded, should not be judged on the basis of theological considerations.

There is much truth in these observations. Not everyone is a trained theologian and is capable of making all of the distinctions and qualifications that theologians regard as important. It would be unfair to ask everyone involved in ministry to expound in detail on various minor points of doctrine or to discuss subtle points of New Testament Greek grammar.

The problem is that certain persons *are* teaching on doctrinal or theological matters beyond their competency. If a person has a calling from God to evangelize but not to teach doctrine, then he or she should not teach doctrine. If a person does teach on theological matters and teaches false doctrine, he or she must be held accountable for it.

Not only are there different kinds of ministries, there are different kinds of teachers. Some people are gifted at teaching how to develop healthy Christian marriages and families. Others are gifted at teaching how to lead others to faith in Christ. Others are gifted at teaching Christian doctrine. Some people may be gifted at teaching in more than one of these areas, but such teachers are rare. There is nothing wrong with a person teaching on marriage and family who is not formally trained in theology. A problem arises only when such a person also tries to teach theology and advocates false doctrine.

James 3:1 says, "Let not many of you become teachers, my brethren, knowing that as such we will incur a stricter judgment." It is one thing to express errant opinions on theological matters in a private setting. It is another to present oneself to the body of Christ as a teacher and then express the same sort of errant opinions. Especially if people write a book, or distribute cassette tapes of their sermons, or publish a newsletter, in which they offer teaching on doctrinal matters, they have to expect to be held accountable for teaching false doctrine.

In some cases, a teacher who is generally sound doctrinally will express a false opinion on doctrine out of sheer ignorance, and once confronted will gladly retract the error. Such a person should not be criticized or labeled a heretic or a false teacher. On the other hand, ignorance cannot excuse continued teaching of false doctrine. A person who is confronted about teaching doctrinal error and who refuses to retract the error cannot legitimately hide behind the disclaimer of not being a theologian. Nor can someone whose doctrinal teaching is generally unsound hide behind such an excuse.

Peter warns that some people who are "untaught and unstable distort" the Scriptures "to their own destruction" (2 Pet. 3:16). The fact that they are "untaught" or ignorant is no excuse. Likewise, Paul warns that there are those who want "to be teachers of the Law, even though they do not understand either what they are saying or the matters about which they make confident assertions" (1 Tim. 1:7). Paul's instruction to Timothy is that he was to tell such persons "not to teach strange doctrines" (1 Tim. 1:3). Later in the same letter Paul states, "If anyone advocates a different doctrine, and does not agree with sound words, those of our Lord Jesus Christ, and with the doctrine conforming to godliness, he is conceited and *understands nothing*" (1 Tim. 6:3–4a). Ignorance is no excuse for continuing to advocate false doctrine.

It might be helpful to think of ignorance as being of two kinds. There is the innocent ignorance of those who are still learning, who realize they have much to learn, and who do not speak confidently or try to instruct others on matters about which they are still ignorant. Such ignorance can be corrected, and even if it continues will do no harm and will deserve no blame. On the other hand, there is the culpable ignorance of those who refuse to bother learning the truth, who think they already know everything of importance on the matter, and who speak confidently or teach others on matters about which they are ignorant and happen to be quite mistaken.

Here is another way of looking at this objection. Excusing a person's false teaching by appealing to his ministry's good results in other respects is another form of the "check the fruit" objection. While we should check the fruit, we should also examine the root.

It is amazing to hear false teachers in the church today being excused by their followers by an appeal to their teachers' ignorance. One would think that if Christians were aware that certain teachers of doctrine were doctrinally ignorant, they would go elsewhere for their doctrine. In some cases these teachers claim not to be ignorant at all, but to be the recipients of new doctrinal insights or even revelations of doctrines that the church supposedly had lost centuries ago. In such cases the excuse of not being theologians rings especially hollow.

"Don't Fight over Words"

Yet another objection to doctrinal discernment is that it is nothing but "fighting over words." The expression comes from 2 Timothy 2:14, where Paul tells Timothy to charge his people "not to wrangle about words, which is useless, and leads to the ruin of the hearers." Some people allege that any criticism of a teacher's doctrine, particularly criticisms that focus on that teacher's use of certain words, should be dismissed as fighting over words.

Certainly many doctrinal disputes are rightly characterized as fighting over words. But by no stretch of the imagination can that be said about *all* doctrinal disputes. In the very same letter in which Paul warns Timothy to avoid fighting over words, he also instructs him to "retain the standard of *sound words* which you have heard from me" (2 Tim. 1:13). Paul clearly expects Timothy to take a stand for the truth of Paul's teaching and against the unsound words of the false teachers.

In fact, immediately after warning Timothy not to fight over words, he exhorts him to make sure that he is "handling accurately the word of truth," and tells him to "avoid worldly and empty chatter" (2:15, 16). Paul then singles out "Hymenaeus and Philetus, men who have gone astray from the truth saying that the resurrection has already taken place, and thus they upset the faith of some" (2:17–18). We might say that the dispute here was over the word *resurrection* and its meaning; but contending for the biblical understanding of this word is not mere "fighting over words."

Ironically, when the meaning or use of certain words is disputed, often it is because false teachers have come along and attached novel meanings to words commonly used in Christian doctrine. Typically, they will assert that the church has misunderstood the biblical doctrine related to this word, and now they are going to set everyone straight. Then, when their misuse or misdefinition of terms is challenged, they will sometimes hide behind the excuse of not wanting to "fight over words"!

"It Won't Send You to Hell"

The final objection to doctrinal discernment we will consider here is this: If believing a certain doctrine won't keep people from being saved—if it is possible to accept it and still be saved—then why should it be rejected? Here's another way of putting it: If Christians can disagree about a certain doctrinal matter and still be Christians, then it is not worth dividing over that doctrine.

This objection assumes what might be called a *minimalist* approach to doctrinal discernment. Those who take this approach can agree that we ought to have some doctrinal standards. However, they want to keep those standards very restricted. Specifically, they want them to include nothing on which a person might disagree and yet still be saved. This minimalist approach might seem reasonable on the surface, but it is based on a false premise. The premise, or assumption, of the argument is that *anyone who might possibly be saved must be regarded as a Christian and a member of the church of Jesus Christ in good standing*. This assumption can be proved false biblically. For example, while it might be possible for a person who has never been baptized to be saved, such a person cannot be regarded as a practicing Christian. The New Testament assumes that all Christians are baptized (Matt. 28:19; Acts 2:38; 1 Cor. 12:13). On another note, a professing Christian involved in gross sin and unrepentant must be disciplined and removed from the church—even though the person might be saved (1 Cor. 5:1–13). Similarly, Christians who persist in promoting false doctrine must be silenced, removed from the church if necessary, even though they might be genuine believers (Titus 1:10–11; 3:10–11).

It might be helpful to remember that we are not supposed to be trying to determine who is saved and who is not. That is a judgment that is beyond our ability to make competently. Our responsibility, as a church, is to be faithful to the truth and standards of God revealed in Scripture. If someone refuses to acknowledge those standards or that truth, even going so far as to contradict the church's biblical teaching, they have in effect cut themselves off from the church. There is nothing harmful or divisive about giving public recognition to that fact. On the other hand, there is something quite harmful about turning a blind eye to the problem. If false teaching is allowed to continue unchecked and unchallenged, it may gain additional support and lead to a more divisive situation later.

If a minimalist standard of doctrine is unworkable, what standard should be used? What doctrines must be accepted for people to be regarded as Christians in good standing? Answering that question is really what the rest of the book is about. The traditional term used to refer to the right standard of doctrine is *orthodoxy*. In the next chapter, we shall consider how best to define this term and its opposite, heresy.

mined is not orthodoxy but confessional fidelity. That is, if someone wishes to be an ordained minister of a particular denomination, that denomination is within its rights to ask that such a person agree with its doctrines. If someone does not (e.g., if someone disagrees with the denomination's position on speaking in tongues or predestination), then that person should not expect to be ordained in such a denomination. Given the present diversity of denominations, this should be expected.

On the other hand, it is lamentable that the church has allowed itself to be divided over nonessential issues. Thus, adherence to a denomination's particular distinctives should not necessarily be made the test of Christian orthodoxy. Of course, some of the doctrinal stands taken by a denomination may be basic to orthodoxy (e.g., a confession of the deity of Jesus Christ). In such cases, the denomination's confession and orthodoxy coincide.

What, then, should be the standard of orthodoxy? And how should it be determined? Perhaps the most troublesome question is, *Who* should determine the standard?

Certainly I do not claim to have any particular authority to determine by what standard orthodoxy shall be judged. I claim no special anointing beyond that which all Christians have (1 John 2:20, 27). I make no claims to apostolic or prophetic authority. I am not even an ordained minister. Who, then, am I to judge who is and is not orthodox? Who am I to call anyone a heretic?

My answer to these questions is twofold. First, *I am a Christian*, and as such have a responsibility to avoid heresy. I also have a responsibility, as part of the church, to warn others of false doctrine, as we saw in chapter 3. I can hardly do so if I do not have some idea as to what heresy is. Second, *I am a teacher*, called by God to the ministry of teaching my fellow Christians sound doctrine. That gives me no special authority or mantle of divine sanction, and I would not want anyone to assume that whatever I say is true. But it does mean that God has given me a special responsibility, and if I am faithful he

will use me to guide other believers into a more complete
and accurate understanding of his truth. If I am truly
faithful, those who are open to God's truth will know that
what I say is true—not because I say it, but simply
because I have led them to see what has always been in
God's Word, the Bible.

Toward Definitions

What, then, is orthodoxy, and what is heresy? First of
all, I wish to point out that the term *orthodoxy* is not in
the Bible. That does not mean that the concept itself is
unbiblical, but that we cannot read off its meaning from
biblical texts.

The words *heresy* and *heretic* are in the Bible, and are
used in somewhat varying senses. The Jews called
Christianity a "heresy" (Acts 24:14), probably meaning
they considered it a sect under God's condemnation. But
Paul refers to the various factions among the Corinthian
Christians as "heresies," that is, "divisions" (1 Cor.
11:19). Here he seems to regard some of these divisions
as distinguishing true believers from false believers, but
other divisions as simply unfortunate expressions of sin-
ful disunity among Christians, without suggesting that all
who belonged to these different factions were lost.
Elsewhere, though, Paul refers to "heresies" or divisions
as works of the flesh (Gal. 5:19–20) and says that a
"heretic"—a person causing divisions in the church—is
perverted and self-condemned (Titus 3:10–11). Finally,
Peter speaks of destructive "heresies" in the sense of doctrines which deny Christ the Lord (2 Pet. 2:1).

From this survey it is evident that a "heresy" in biblical
terminology could be merely an unfortunate division
among Christians, but in a stricter sense is a divisive
teaching or practice destructive of genuine faith and
deserving of condemnation. The looser sense corresponds
to our modern denominations, while the stricter sense
applies most clearly to groups which reject basic Christian

doctrines and set themselves apart from the historic church in its many forms. But a "heresy" in the latter sense can have its start, at least, within the church. Whenever heresies in this strict sense arise, Christians are called to separate themselves from those who persist in holding them.

We may therefore define "heresy" in the strict sense as *a teaching which directly opposes the essentials of the Christian faith, so that true Christians must divide themselves from those who hold it.* Note the difference here: a "faction" or heresy in the looser sense is an unfortunate division separating Christians from one another, and Christians are called to do whatever they can to overcome these divisions (1 Cor. 1:10). But a heresy in the stricter sense is a division separating Christians from non-Christians (or, at best, from Christians who are persisting in grave error), and Christians are called to draw the line and refuse to have spiritual fellowship with those who cross over it. This is not to say that Christians should not show genuine love, compassion, and personal respect for heretics; too often in church history "heretic" has been a hate-word.

How, then, should we define "orthodoxy"? We might define it as *that body of essential teachings which must be held by all those who would be accepted as Christians.* To put it simply, whatever religious teachings and practices are not heretical are orthodox, and vice versa.

Notice that we have not said that all members of churches which teach heresy are lost. This is no more true than saying that all who are members of churches which teach orthodoxy are saved. In saying that people are heretics, or that they are following heresy, we are not pronouncing judgment on their eternal souls. We *are* saying that if they follow those heresies consistently, they will certainly be lost. Conversely, in saying that someone is orthodox we are not saying that they are necessarily true Christians with the assurance of eternal life. We *are* saying that if they follow orthodox doctrine as the basis of their life (and thus trust in Christ alone for their right standing before God) they will be saved.

6

It's Not Always Black or White

*I*t might seem that doctrinal discernment should be a fairly cut-and-dried procedure of determining whether a doctrine is orthodox or heretical. After all, we have defined orthodoxy and heresy in such a way that they seem to cover all possibilities.

Either a doctrine is such that those who hold it should be accepted as Christians (in which case it is orthodox), or it is not (in which case it is heretical). This might seem to imply a black-or-white approach in which all doctrine is either completely orthodox or completely heretical.

Although doctrinal discernment would be a lot neater and simpler if this were the case, unfortunately things are more complicated.

Black and White Make Gray

A single doctrine is never held in isolation from other doctrines, but rather is always part of a system or network of beliefs held by a person or group. And sometimes that system of beliefs includes many doctrines which are orthodox as well as some which are heretical. For example, a religious group might hold that the Bible is the Word of God, that there is only one God, and that Jesus was born of a virgin and rose from the dead, and yet deny the deity of Jesus Christ. Such a group's *belief system* is heretical, even though it contains many true *beliefs*.

Moreover, a group's heretical beliefs generally lead them to misunderstand or misapply even those true beliefs they do confess, since the beliefs tend to be interdependent and thus mutually affect one another.

Thus, one of the tasks of doctrinal discernment is to sort out which beliefs in a heretical system are actually heretical, which are not, and how the nonheretical beliefs are misapplied because of the heretical system in which they are held.

Black on White Also Makes Gray

The second sort of complication to be noticed is that people often hold conflicting beliefs. Because people are often inconsistent, in some cases they may hold to orthodox beliefs but also hold to beliefs that undermine or contradict their orthodox beliefs. The difficulty presented in such cases is to sort out whether the belief system is basically orthodox or not.

For example, many professing Christian groups today confess belief in one God, but also speak of human beings (usually Christians in particular) as being in some sense "gods." This verbal contradiction may or may not betray a real contradiction in the substance of their beliefs. The fact is that these different groups mean vastly different things by calling believers "gods." In some cases it is evident that they really do not believe in one God at all. In other cases it is clear that they are using the word *gods* of believers in a figurative sense such that their confession of one God is not contradicted at all. In still other cases a real tension exists, and it is difficult to avoid concluding that the group in question holds conflicting views.

Aberrational Doctrine

It is helpful to speak of religious doctrines which undermine or are in tension with a group's orthodox beliefs as *aberrational* or *aberrant*. Holding such aberrational views is a serious problem, and those who do so must be considered as being in serious sin and should be treated accordingly. Specifically, those advocating such errors should not be allowed to teach or minister in the church, and those refusing to keep such aberrant views to themselves should be excommunicated.

The charge that a person's or group's beliefs are aberrational is a serious one that cannot be made easily. It is arguable that at one level any incorrect belief is at tension with or undermines orthodox beliefs. By aberrational, however, I am referring only to false beliefs which do serious damage to the integrity of an orthodox confession of faith.

Unsound Doctrine

One would think that the categories of orthodox, aberrational, and heretical would be sufficient. And if all one is concerned about is a measure of orthodoxy, these categories are enough.

However, the waters are muddied even further by the fact that doctrines are often taught in the church which do not seem to impinge much at all on orthodoxy, yet are so bad that they deserve to be rejected. If aberrational doctrine is "gray," perhaps this kind of doctrine might be colored "brown." It isn't good, sound doctrine, nor is it outright heresy, nor is it a mixture of orthodox and unorthodox views. It's just unhealthy, inappropriate doctrine.

The apostle Paul had to criticize such doctrine. He told Timothy to "instruct certain men not to teach strange doctrines, nor to pay attention to myths and endless genealogies" (1 Tim. 1:3–4a). These doctrines were to be rejected, not because they would lead anyone to destruction, but because they provoked only "speculation" and did not further God's work and purposes (v. 4b). These bad doctrines missed the point; they produced "fruitless discussion" instead of love and faith (vv. 5–6).

Doctrinal discernment is needed, not just to determine what doctrine is barely acceptable and what is not, but to determine what doctrine is *good*, what doctrine furthers God's work in the world in and through the church. In the school of Christian doctrine, it is not sufficient to get a barely passing grade (a D-minus instead of an F!). Such poor doctrine should be rejected by the church in favor of good, sound doctrine.

The church today is plagued, not only by heresies and aberrations, but by doctrines which I would characterize as "junk-food doctrine." Junk food won't kill you, unless that's all you eat—in which case poor nutrition will eventually catch up with you. Junk-food doctrine is not good, nor is it really bad. You might call it "flaky" doctrine.

Some examples would really help here, but I wish to keep my pledge not to give specific examples so that people can learn the principles set forth here without prejudice. So let me make one up. (I cannot guarantee that no one really believes this, but I've never heard of anyone who did!) Suppose someone believed that each book of the Old Testament corresponded to a specific end-time event. In this theory, there are thirty-nine events which must take place in the last generation before Christ's return, and these thirty-nine events will take place in the same order as the thirty-nine books of the Old Testament supposedly foreshadows them. Then all we have to do is see which of the thirty-nine events have allegedly taken place and which have not, and we can pinpoint what must take place still before Christ's return. And suppose that this theory is made the key to "unlocking" the teaching of the Old Testament. Pretty wild, you say? Well, there are a lot of teachings circulating in the church today which come uncomfortably close to this one. (Speculations about the end-times account for a high percentage of junk-food doctrines in the church today.) You can see that there doesn't seem to be anything overtly harmful about this theory. But nor does the theory have anything to offer of value. For one thing, it's false (I just made it up, after all). It is not the key to the meaning or structure of the Old Testament. At best, this teaching would distract Christians from the business of truly understanding and applying the Old Testament to their lives.

Discernment as an Art

The phenomenon of such flaky or junk-food doctrine points up the difficulty involved in doctrinal discernment. If doctrines can be black or white, gray or brown, then it is evident that doctrinal discernment is a matter of fine judgment indeed. We tend to think of it as a matter of having three or four boxes, each clearly labeled "orthodox," "heretical," and so forth, and deciding in which box to put each doctrine. Sometimes, perhaps much of the time, it is that easy. But in some ways it is more like locating a doctrine along a continuum. At one extreme are doctrines that are clearly orthodox, at the other doctrines that are clearly heretical. But somewhere toward the middle there are doctrines which are less easily pigeonholed.

Does this mean that we throw up our hands and give up? Does it mean that we treat with suspicion anyone who attempts to make such judgments? No, since we have already seen that God commands us to exercise discernment.

The sum of the matter is that doctrinal discernment is a difficult task—one which requires sensitivity, a sense of proportion and balance, and a deep understanding of what is essential and what is not. It is less like a cut-and-dried problem in physics or arithmetic and more like an art. (I do not mean to deny that at a certain level scientists and mathematicians also can exercise artistic talents.) New heresies and aberrations are constantly arising, as well as new insights into biblical truth, and discernment is needed to tell the difference. Thus, the task of doctrinal discernment is an ongoing necessity in the Christian church.

Having shown that doctrinal discernment is necessary, I have yet to say very much at all about how it is to be done. That will be the focus of Part Two.

Part TWO

Guidelines for Doctrinal Discernment

7

Principles for Identifying Heresy

iscerning orthodoxy from heresy should be done on the basis of sound principles, each of which in turn must be based on the teaching of God's Word. I begin, then, by discussing four principles which the church ought to utilize as tools to identify and expose heresy. Although they are subject to misunderstanding and abuse, all four—properly interpreted—are valid and should be utilized together in doctrinal discernment.

The Protestant Principle

Here I am not referring to an exclusively Protestant position, but rather to a principle that will be especially agreeable to Protestants (particularly evangelicals). For this reason I call this the protestant (with a small *p*) principle. According to this principle, *the Bible alone is the written Word of God, and as such is the only infallible, definitive standard in matters of controversy in the church.* This principle follows from the teaching of Jesus Christ himself, who taught that while human tradition and religious leaders are fallible, Scripture is the Word of God and never errs (Matt. 5:17–20; 15:3–9; 22:29; John 10:35). Since to be a Christian means, minimally, to be a follower of Jesus Christ, no person or group can claim to be faithfully Christian who does not acknowledge this special authority of the Bible.

I said that this teaching is not held exclusively by Protestants, although it is especially agreeable to them. Both Roman Catholicism and Eastern Orthodoxy (the other two main branches of Christianity) teach that the church's traditions are infallible and authoritative, a teaching with which Protestants cannot agree. Thus, these branches of Christianity do not adhere fully to the protestant principle as defined here. On the other hand, Catholicism and Orthodoxy do teach that the Bible is the *norma normans*, that is, the norm by which all other norms are to be judged. Thus, at least in some sense, the view of all major Christian traditions is that Scripture has the final word. But evangelical Protestants, I believe, have upheld this principle more consistently than Christians in the Catholic or Orthodox traditions.

On the other hand, liberalism—which began in main-line Protestantism and has virtually engulfed it, and which has now made significant inroads in Roman Catholicism—completely denies the protestant principle. Liberalism presumes to judge the teachings of the Bible according to the canons of human reason. Accordingly, it should be rejected as apostate by true believers of all major Christian traditions.

The protestant principle has often been summarized by the Protestant Reformation motto *sola scriptura* ("only Scripture"). Taken in its true sense, this means that only Scripture is an unerring verbal expression of the mind of God for the church prior to Christ's return. Unfortunately, the doctrine of *sola scriptura* is often misunderstood and misapplied in our day. Often the "Bible-only" kind of approach criticized by Catholic and Orthodox Christians is actually a distortion of the protestant principle. So let me specify very clearly what *sola scriptura* does not mean.

First of all, the protestant principle should not be interpreted to mean that truth can be found only in Scripture. There are many truths—mathematical, scientific, historical, psychological, and other sorts of truths—that are not found specifically in the Bible. All such truths, if indeed they are truths and not mistaken notions, must cohere with the Bible. Sometimes our knowledge of the Bible will lead us to correct our mistaken notions about history or science or psychology. On the other hand, sometimes advances in our knowledge in these fields will force us to reexamine and refine, even correct, our understanding of the Bible. This happened, for example, when Galileo proved that the earth revolves around the sun and therefore that the earth moves, contrary to the standard interpretations of the Bible at that time. The motto "all truth is God's truth" is itself true. Granted sometimes people accept as true theories and speculations that are not, but that is an abuse.

A simplistic "Bible-only" application of the protestant principle that refuses to allow such corrections to our understanding of Scripture is destructive, in two ways. First, it divides Christians, because those who are open to all truth will not allow themselves to be held back by those who are closed to anything that will not fit their set interpretations of the Bible. Second, it hampers evangelism, because intelligent non-Christians can see that such "Bible-only" fundamentalism blinds its adherents to proven truth, and this discourages them from taking Christianity seriously.

Second, the protestant principle does not mean that all traditions are based on falsehood. Traditions that cannot be found in the Bible are not thereby proved false. To prove a tradition false, it must be shown to *contradict* the

Bible. If this cannot be done, then the tradition must be evaluated on the basis of the historical evidence for its authenticity. For example, the Bible never identifies explicitly any of the authors of the four Gospels. However, that does not invalidate the traditions that they were written by Matthew, Mark, Luke, and John.

On the other hand, traditions that cannot be substantiated from the Bible should not be made binding on Christians. That is, Christians should not be required to accept as dogmas traditions that do not have biblical warrant. This is the aspect of the protestant principle that is most troublesome to Catholics. However, at least some Catholic apologists and theologians do maintain that all Catholic dogmas have some warrant in Scripture for them, even if they cannot be proved directly from Scripture. This is an area in which Protestants and Catholics need to pursue further dialogue.

Third, the protestant principle should not be interpreted to forbid using words not found in the Bible to express biblical doctrine. For example, the idea that the Bible is a "canon," or rule of faith, is biblical even though the word *canon* is not found in the Bible. The idea that God is "self-existent," meaning that his existence depends on nothing other than himself, is biblical even though the word *self-existent* is not in the Bible.

A related point is that necessary deductions or inferences from the Bible are as normative as the statements of the Bible themselves. That is, any statement that logically follows from the express statements of Scripture is just as true and binding as the statements of the Bible themselves. For example, once we understand that the biblical statements that *God is not a man* and *God is spirit* (among many other statements in Scripture) logically imply the statement *God is incorporeal* (that is, God does not have a body), then to be faithful to Scripture we must agree that God is incorporeal. It is perfectly valid for the church to require, as a test of orthodoxy, that Christians confess that God is incorporeal, even though this statement is never found in the Bible. (By the way, this statement is speaking of God in his eternal divine nature, and does not deny that God became incarnate in a bodily form in Jesus Christ.)

I have devoted considerable attention to the protestant principle because it is, in my view, foundational for the others. This is not simply a bias on my part. Rather, as I shall try to explain, the protestant principle must be held as a foundational premise or assumption if the other three principles are to be understood correctly. I do not wish to imply that one must accept the protestant principle, just as I have explained it, to be a Christian (although a complete rejection of biblical authority is heresy). However, I do maintain that sound doctrinal discernment, to be put on a solid footing, must be based on this principle.

The Evangelical Principle

In Europe, "evangelical" is often synonymous with "Lutheran," and the principle I enunciate here will be especially agreeable to that tradition, although certainly transcending it. According to this principle, *whatever is contrary to the gospel of Jesus Christ is to be rejected as heresy*. This principle is based directly on such passages as Galatians 1:6–9 and 1 Corinthians 15:1–4. Here, "the gospel" refers not to the Bible in its entirety, but to its central message of reconciliation of human beings to God through the redemptive work of Christ.

This principle implies that not every misinterpretation of or departure from the Bible is equally damaging to authentic Christian faith. Misunderstanding the relationship between the Millennium and the Second Coming, for example, is not as serious an error as misunderstanding the relationship between faith and works. Denying that Jonah escaped alive after being inside a large fish for three days is not as bad an error as denying that Jesus rose from the grave after being dead for three days. Whether the errors are clear-cut or debatable from our perspective, it remains true that some errors are worse than others.

On the other hand, this principle can be misapplied by treating the gospel as a "canon within the canon" such that some parts of the Bible become more authoritative than others. While we may draw more directly on the Gospel of John or the Epistle to the Romans in our presentation of the gospel, our understanding of the gospel should be shaped by the entire Bible. Some extreme or aberrant groups have lost sight of this and have argued that only one part of the Bible—say, the Book of Acts—presents the gospel of salvation. Besides being contrary to the facts (e.g., Paul rehearses the basics of the gospel in 1 Cor. 15:1–8), such an argument undermines the unity of Scripture.

Moreover, even seemingly less important errors can be symptomatic of outright heretical beliefs. For example, while some variant views on the Millennium are tolerable among Christians, other views should be regarded as heretical, such as the view that the Millennium will be a period in which unbelievers will be raised and given a second chance to save themselves by doing good works. Clearly this view is heretical because of its bearing on the doctrine of salvation. The belief that Jonah was not swallowed by a fish and then set free three days later might be symptomatic of a prejudice against all miracles. On the other hand, some Christians who freely confess that God could have done such a miracle hold that the Book of Jonah is a parable and was simply not intended as history. The latter view may be wrong, but it is not anti-Christian in the way the former view clearly is.

Finally, it should be noted that in mainline denominations heavily influenced by liberalism, the "gospel" has typically been reinterpreted and watered down to the point of no longer being the biblical gospel at all. The evangelical principle must always be tied to the protestant principle and not pitted against it, as is the case in liberal Protestantism.

MACRO TRADITION
NORMA NORMANDA

The Orthodox Principle

I call this principle the "orthodox" principle because it will be especially agreeable to Christians in the Orthodox (Eastern) tradition. According to this principle, *the creeds of the undivided church should be regarded as reliable expressions of the essential truths on which they speak.* This principle follows from the biblical teaching that the Christian faith was delivered once for all to the saints (Jude 3) and that the gates of Hades would not prevail against the church (Matt. 16:18). These texts (see also Matt. 28:20; John 14:26; Eph. 4:11–16) make it inconceivable that the whole church could establish as *normative* what is in fact aberrant or heretical.

Thus, the creeds formulated by the early church before it split into Eastern Orthodoxy, Roman Catholicism, and Protestantism, and accepted by *all three branches* of Christianity, should be regarded as reliable standards by which heresies may be exposed. Such creeds as the Nicene and Chalcedonian Creeds—which speak of the Father, Son, and Holy Spirit as one God (the Trinity) and of Jesus Christ as uniquely God and man (the incarnation)—expressed the faith of all Christians when they were written, and have unified all Christians against heresy for centuries. They are therefore deserving of respect and should be honored as tools for identifying and exposing heresy.

MONOPHYSITISM
NESTORIANISM.

Note that I am not saying that Christians cannot choose to disagree with some of the precise wording of these creeds. After all, they are not infallible, inspired documents. Nor am I saying that those churches which choose not to use the creeds, or which have little or no regard for creeds as such, are heretical. Rather, I am simply saying that a doctrine or belief should be regarded as heretical if it departs from the essential, substantial teachings of these creeds. I am therefore adopting a more flexible form of this principle than is actually held by Eastern Orthodox Christians themselves. I am also pleading with my anticreedal brothers and sisters in Christ to rethink their rejection of these fine expressions of orthodoxy.

The Catholic Principle

By "catholic" I do not mean specifically Roman Catholic, but simply "universal" (which is what the Greek word *katholikos* means). The notion of "catholicity" has been much abused, but it has also been ignored; both stances are unfortunate. The catholic principle is that *any doctrine that contradicts what the church as a whole (in all times and places) has regarded as essential to the faith should be considered heretical.* This principle also follows from the biblical teaching mentioned above that God will keep the whole church from heresy.

It should be noted that this principle is a generalization, not an absolutely definitive test. I say this because by the "whole" church I do not mean every last individual in the church, as if the dissent of one or a few professing Christians could negate a doctrine's status as "catholic." The principle rather seeks to uphold what the vast majority of those who have participated in the church's worship, in all its various branches and denominations, and who have upheld the faith as defined by the orthodox principle, have regarded as essential or basic to their faith.

Moreover, the catholic principle—properly understood—presupposes the protestant principle. That is, when we speak of "the church" in all times and places, we are speaking of that community of faith which regards the Bible as the supreme norm of its faith. We are thus excluding from the outset those segments of Christendom that have abandoned faith in the Bible as the Word of God. It has only been in the last two centuries that large segments of Christendom within both Protestantism and Catholicism have denied absolute biblical authority. And in the vast majority of such cases, the doctrines of the Trinity, the incarnation, and the atonement have been rejected as well. These segments of Christendom must be regarded as apostate, having fallen away from the faith.

These considerations are helpful in making more precise the notion of appealing to the position of the "historic Christian church" as a litmus test of orthodoxy. What we ought to mean by this expression is the Bible-believing community of faith as it has existed continuously throughout the centuries. Those segments of Christendom which have introduced new doctrinal revelations, or which have rejected biblical authority, are by this definition not part of the historic Christian church.

Finally, note that not everything that has been believed by most Christians falls under the catholic principle, but only those things that the church has held to be *essential*. In other words, we need to distinguish between necessary, essential beliefs and customary, nonessential beliefs. For the first fifteen centuries of church history, virtually all Christians held that the earth was at the physical center of the universe. But by no means does this make that erroneous belief part of the "catholic" or universal Christian faith. Here the "evangelical principle" is a valuable corrective to a possible misapplication of the catholic principle.

What Is Doctrine?

So much has been said already about doctrine that it might seem obvious that we know what we are talking about when we use the word *doctrine*. However, some reflection on the nature of doctrine will be very helpful in coming to grips with the task of doctrinal discernment.

Understanding what doctrine is, and is not, is essential if doctrine is to be neither overexalted nor undervalued. Many disagreements about the relative importance of certain doctrinal matters are rooted, I am convinced, in a failure to appreciate the nature of doctrine. The nature of Christian doctrine can be discussed under three headings. Doctrine, properly understood, is (1) propositional, (2) polemical, and (3) perspectival.

Doctrine as Propositional

Doctrine is the formulation of Christian faith in propositional form. A *proposition*, as defined here, is a statement that makes a declaration of fact. A proposition asserts, "This is the way things are," or, "This is what happened," or, "This is what that means," or the like.

Not everything in the Bible is propositional. For one thing, the Bible contains other kinds of sentences, such as questions and commands. Furthermore, the genre, or type of writing, in which much of the Bible is written is not typically propositional in form. For example, narratives and poetry do not generally contain many direct propositional statements. As is well known, the Old Testament is largely composed of writings of these two genres.

Recognizing the fact that doctrine is just one way to express Christian faith is crucial to appreciating its importance and its limitations. On the one hand, doctrine acts as a kind of control on our understanding of nonpropositional expressions of faith. Even within the Bible itself, we use the more overtly doctrinal portions to interpret the narratives and poetry. For example, we use Leviticus and Deuteronomy to evaluate the actions of the kings in 1 and 2 Kings. We use the epistles of Paul and Peter to help us learn what in the Book of Acts is a normative practice and what is a unique historical occurrence. Outside the Bible we use Christian doctrine as a check on such nondoctrinal or semidoctrinal expressions of faith as gospel lyrics, church dramas, and liturgy. Doctrine can be invaluable in keeping such artistic expressions of faith "on track" in the beliefs and values they convey to others.

On the other hand, propositional expressions of doctrine have some limitations. They are better at conveying ideas than feelings. They are better at stating abstract truths than telling stories. In recent years some theologians have even been pressing for the church to focus more on "narrative theology" than on abstract, systematic formulations of doctrine. A renewed emphasis on the narration of biblical events is a good thing, as long as we do not lose sight of three things. (1) Those events in the Bible's narratives really happened. (2) The events are narrated to reveal to us truths about God and our relationship with him that exceed a simple recounting of the events. (3) The Bible mixes narrative and other nondoctrinal forms of communication with doctrinal instruction, both in the Old Testament and in the New.

Doctrine as Polemical

While the statement that doctrine is propositional might bring only a yawn, as obvious as it is, the statement that doctrine is by nature polemical might provoke some raised eyebrows. Saying that doctrine is polemical will imply to many that it is purely negative and argumentative. Shouldn't doctrine be positive, uplifting, edifying? Must it always be polemical?

Certainly in expressing our Christian beliefs we need not always be overtly polemicizing against the beliefs of others. Again, there are legitimate, even indispensable alternative ways to express one's faith other than in doctrine. However, strange as it may sound at first, it is very important to understand that doctrine is fundamentally polemical.

How is this so? Well, Christian faith is first and foremost a personal relationship between human beings (both individually and corporately) and the personal God revealed in Jesus Christ. It is the story of God's creation of the human race, our rebellion against God, and his merciful work of redemption culminating in the death and resurrection of Jesus. The purpose of doctrinal formulation—of putting together formalized expressions of the truths of the Christian faith—is to ensure the integrity of that faith against misconstruals and distortions of those truths. In short, good doctrine is necessitated by the existence of bad doctrine.

One can see this throughout the doctrinal portions of the New Testament. The Gospels are full of discourses in which Jesus refutes misinterpretations of the Old Testament by the scribes and Pharisees. Jesus' teaching also frequently rebuts erroneous understanding of the significance of his miraculous works. In his epistles Paul is frequently combatting false teachings about everything from circumcision to sex to the resurrection. Hebrews, Peter's epistles, John's epistles, and Jude all deal polemically with errors of various sorts.

The pervasiveness of polemic in the doctrinal portions of the New Testament (the same may be found in the Old) has some important lessons for us. Christians who polemicize against false or distorted versions of Christian doctrine are simply following the biblical example. Concern for doctrinal accuracy, and opposition to false doctrine, are trademarks of a sound, biblically minded Christian. The pietistic notion that negative expressions of doctrine are unloving and unedifying is foreign to the Bible.

Another extremely important lesson to be learned is that if Christian doctrine seems too complicated, generally the level of technicality is due to the fact that the biblical doctrine in question has been the object of considerable attack. Careful qualified statements about the deity of Christ, for example, become necessary only when people come along who claim to be Christians but who deny or distort the truth of his deity. As cruder denials of biblical truth are refuted by Christian theologians and the church is made aware of those denials, more subtle denials of the same truths tend to take their place. These more subtle denials call forth new refutations, hopefully (not always, unfortunately) equally subtle and accurate in response. This cycle has in many cases repeated over the centuries. That is why some of the doctrinal controversies in the church today seem to be over minor issues, even though they are not.

Although heresies tend to become increasingly subtle, the essential issues never become too difficult for lay Christians to understand. I have never encountered a heretical teaching which could not be shown to the satisfaction of lay Christians to be unbiblical and destructive of authentic Christian faith. The philosophical assumptions or interpretive fine points may sometimes be too arcane for the layperson to understand, but the basic theological, spiritual, or ethical error does not escape them.

Doctrine as Perspectival

The third point to be made about doctrine is that it is *perspectival.* What I mean here is that although truth is a unity and is absolute, our human understanding and doctrinal expression of truth are always partial, incomplete, and less than comprehensive, and in that sense might even be called "relative." This is not relativ*ism.* Relativism says that all *truth* is relative. Perspectivalism, as I mean it, says that truth is absolute, but our *knowledge* of the truth is always relative. That is, it is always *our* knowledge, seen from our vantage point, understood within the context of our experiences and opportunities for gaining knowledge.

Moreover, doctrine is perspectival in that it uses language which, because of its very nature, cannot give us an absolutely comprehensive account of the truth. Doctrinal language can be true and expressive of absolute truth; this is true of the Bible's use of language through and through. But no doctrinal language, even that found in the Bible, is exhaustive of the truth. The Bible tells us nothing but truth, and it tells us all that we need to know to live according to God's will; but it does not tell us everything, and it does not exhaustively state the truth even on the subjects it covers. (For example, the Bible tells us much about the historical times and places related to Christ's birth, but it does not furnish us with an exact date of his birth.)

Much less, then, should we expect any of our fallible human doctrinal formulations to represent the "last word" on any subject. What a creed or confession says about the Trinity, for example, may be quite true, but that does not mean that there is nothing left to say about the Trinity. We will always need to interpret the doctrine of the Trinity afresh as each new generation asks somewhat different questions about it, or the same questions in different words.

The implications of the perspectival nature of doctrine are very important. Because there is always more that could be said about a particular doctrinal matter, and because the same truths can be expressed in different ways, not all doctrinal controversies are a simple matter of determining who's right and who's wrong. Sometimes both parties might be right, because they are expressing the same truths in different words. Perhaps both parties are partly right and partly wrong. In that case, both parties can and should learn from each other.

In other words, we should not assume that people are heretical merely because they express their beliefs in somewhat different words. Nor should we assume that they are orthodox merely because they use the same words as we do. They might mean something different by them.

Moreover, even when we are convinced that people are teaching error, we should seek to learn from them. What aspect of Christian truth are they exploiting? Perhaps there is some facet of biblical truth that the orthodox are ignoring. Perhaps the orthodox have not faced up to explaining orthodox doctrine in the light of some modern scientific discoveries or technological advances. If heretics distort orthodox doctrine in the process of trying to relate it to modern culture, we must express our disagreement and concern; but at the same time, we should take their effort as a signal that those of us who are orthodox have some intellectual work to do.

God is sovereign. He is in control, even of heretics. That does *not* mean that we allow heretics to go on teaching false doctrine in the church unhindered. It does mean, however, that we do not merely thumb our noses at heretics and tell them to get out. If, after we have engaged in dialogue with them, they refuse to repent of their errors, we will have to go our separate ways. But if we are truly open to everything God wants to teach us, we will have learned something from them. In fact, throughout church history God has used heretics to spur the church to greater and greater doctrinal maturity. We can rejoice in this fact, just as we rejoice in knowing that God can use evil for good (Gen. 50:20), indeed, that he works all things together for good for those who love him (Rom. 8:28).

9

Kinds of Heretical Doctrine

*T*aking the protestant principle to heart, we turn now directly to the Bible. What kinds of heretical doctrine does it discuss and forewarn us about? The Bible makes frequent reference to false teachings and it is often within the context of refuting heresy that its positive doctrinal material is cast.

The Old Testament contains solemn warnings against anyone who prophesies or proclaims teachings in the name of any god but the LORD, Jehovah (Deut. 13:1–5; 18:20–22). This is the assumed context in which the New Testament teaching about heresies is framed.

In the New Testament, there are warnings about false prophets (Matt. 24:11, 24; 2 Pet. 2:1)—that is, those who make predictions in the name of God and whose predictions turn out to be false (cf. Deut. 18:22). There is also a warning about false apostles (2 Cor. 11:13). There are warnings about those claiming to be the Christ, or claiming that Christ has come, or that the Day of the Lord has come, or that the resurrection has occurred—when all these events will be so plain and conspicuous that no one will miss them (Matt. 24:5, 23–27; 2 Thess. 2:1–2; 2 Tim. 2:16–18).

There are also warnings about those who proclaim another Jesus or a different gospel, or who introduce a spirit other than God's Spirit (1 Cor. 15:3–5; 2 Cor. 11:4; Gal. 1:6–9). The teaching that circumcision and keeping the Law are necessary for salvation is condemned (Gal. 5:2–4; Phil. 3:2). On the other side, teaching that liberty in Christ gives us excuse for licentiousness is also condemned (Jude 4).

The Nine Enemies of Truth

1. False gospels	2 Cor. 11:4; Gal. 1:6–9	
2. False doctrines	Rom. 16:17; 1 Tim. 1:3	
3. False miracles	Matt. 24:24; 2 Thess. 2:9	
4. False gods	Deut. 13:2; 2 Thess. 2:4	
5. False christs	Matt. 24:24; 2 Cor. 11:4	
6. False spirits	2 Cor. 11:4; 1 John 4:1–2	
7. False prophets	Matt. 24:24; 2 Pet. 2:1	
8. False apostles	2 Cor. 11:13; Rev. 2:2	
9. False teachers	1 Tim. 1:7; 2 Pet. 2:1	

The denial of Jesus Christ's coming in the flesh is regarded as from the spirit of antichrist (1 John 4:1–6). There are warnings about people who cause dissensions by teaching doctrine directly opposed to what Christians already know to be true (Rom. 16:17; Titus 3:10–11). There are warnings about those who claim to love God but do not love God's people (1 John 4:20; 5:1), and who deliberately break away from the church on the basis of perverted doctrine (1 John 2:19). Finally, there are warnings against adding to or taking away from the words of prophetic Scripture (Rev. 22:18–19) or twisting the Scriptures (2 Pet. 3:16).

Looking over these warnings from Scripture, we may classify heresies into six major categories: (1) Heresies about *revelation*—teachings that distort, deny, or add to Scripture in a way that leads people to destruction; false claims to apostolic or prophetic authority. (2) Heresies about *God*—teachings that promote false gods or idolatrous distortions of the true God. (3) Heresies about *Christ*—denials of his unique Lordship, his genuine humanity, his true identity. (4) Heresies about *salvation*—teaching legalism or licentiousness; denying the gospel of Christ's death and resurrection; and so forth. (5) Heresies about the *church*—deliberate attempts to lead people away from the fellowship of true Christians; utter rejection of the church. (6) Heresies about the *future*—false predictions for which divine authority is claimed; claims that Christ's return has taken place; and the like.

Note that errors in any one of these six categories tend to introduce errors into the other five. Take, for instance, the heretical view held by many groups that the church became totally apostate in the early centuries and thus had to be "restored" in the last days. This doctrine implies (1) that Scripture is not a sufficient revelation, but needs supplementing or "explaining" by some authoritative teacher or publication. It also almost always serves as a basis for rejecting the early church's views of (2) God and (3) Christ. Since the Reformation is rejected as falling short of the needed restoration, (4) the doctrine of salvation by grace through faith is likewise rejected. And the doctrine of a restoration comes to dominate the group's views of (6) the future, as it requires them to view many or most biblical prophecies about the future as finding fulfillment in their own group.

We find then that an error in any area of doctrine can affect every other area. Therefore, although heresies tend to fall directly into one or more of these six major categories, heresies can in fact occur on virtually any doctrinal subject. For example, someone who teaches that angels should be worshiped is teaching a heretical view

(Col. 2:18), even though the subject matter is angels. This is because worship of any creature completely cuts the heart out of any confession of God as the one God.

Nor should it be thought that the New Testament gives us a complete catalogue of all possible heresies. In our day there are literally thousands of clever distortions of Christian theology that deserve the label *heresy*, and they can be seen as such apart from being explicitly anticipated and identified as heretical in the Bible. The Bible teaches us what is absolutely essential, enunciates principles as to what is basic to sound Christian faith and what is nonessential, gives us a wide variety of examples of heresies, and expects us to exercise *discernment* in evaluating new and controversial teachings when they surface.

Furthermore, it must be realized that as the church progresses through history and deepens its understanding of Scripture, heresies in general are becoming more subtle, more deceiving, more easily mistaken for authentic Christianity.

For example, modern-day heretics who reject the Old Testament are rarely as frank about it as the second-century heretic Marcion, who simply denied that the Old Testament was in any sense Scripture (he also discarded much of the New Testament). Instead, they adopt a method of interpretation which, while formally admitting that the Bible is God's Word, in effect makes the Old Testament irrelevant to the Christian, which is contrary to the clear teaching of the New Testament (Rom. 15:4; 2 Tim. 3:16).

In short, heresy is any doctrine which the Bible explicitly labels as destructive, damning error; or any doctrine which the Bible instructs is not to be tolerated in the church; or any doctrine which, even if not mentioned in the Bible, utterly contradicts those truths which the Bible indicates are essential for sound Christian faith.

Aberrational views can also be classified according to the above six categories. In each case, the aberrant doctrine seriously compromises the Bible's essential teaching in one or more of those six areas, although not outright denying it.

For example, the practice of speculating on the precise date of the return of Christ can often be an aberration that stops short of heresy. The practice is certainly unbiblical, and in the context of heretical systems of doctrine such date setting can itself be regarded as heretical. But in some cases, teachers have argued more modestly that Christ might return on a certain date, admitting the very real possibility of error, and urging only intensified obedience to God's Word. Even this sort of teaching should be regarded as more or less aberrant, since it violates the biblical warnings against making predictions of this sort; but it is not of itself heretical.

10

A Short Course
on Sound Doctrine

t is impossible in one short chapter to do justice to the totality of orthodox, sound Christian doctrine. What can be done is to introduce the fundamentals of sound doctrine. In this chapter I will not be *arguing* for these doctrines, but simply *presenting* them.

In working through these doctrines, I want to emphasize two things. The first is the importance of these doctrines. Why should these doctrines be regarded as so important that those who dissent from them must be excluded from the fellowship of believers in Jesus Christ? I hope to give some kind of answer to that question as we go along. Second, I want to stress the <u>interconnectedness</u> of these doctrines. If you reject one major aspect of Christian doctrine, it will tend to show up elsewhere in the system. I hope to provide a glimpse of that unity through this all too brief summary.

Revelation

God, in some way, reveals himself to all human beings. The knowledge of God as the Creator and Moral Lawgiver of all is available to all through creation and conscience (Rom. 1:19–20). God also reveals himself to man through direct verbal communication (Gen. 1:29–30; 2:16–17). However, because sin has blinded the human race spiritually (Rom. 1:18, 21–23; 3:10–18), we are now critically in need of God's verbal communication.

This redemptive revealed word of God has come at various times and places through prophets (Heb. 1:1) and was climaxed in the coming of his Son, Jesus Christ (Heb. 1:2), who is the Word incarnate (John 1:1, 14). Both before and after the coming of Jesus Christ, the word of God was put into written form under the guidance of the Holy Spirit (2 Tim. 3:16; 2 Pet. 1:20–21). The resulting Scriptures reveal all of the knowledge that is necessary for salvation and right living (2 Tim. 3:15–17). The Scriptures are absolutely true and without error (Matt. 5:17–18; John 10:35).

Through the Christian apostles and prophets of the first generation of the church, Christ laid a foundation for the ongoing ministry of the church as a united body of Jews and Gentiles (Eph. 2:20; 3:5–6; 4:11–16). The teachings of the Old Testament prophets and the New Testament apostles, preserved reliably for us only in Scripture, are to be the standard by which we judge all doctrinal controversies after the passing of the apostles (2 Pet. 1:19–21; 3:1–2; Jude 17).

New doctrinal revelations, therefore, comparable to those given to the prophets and apostles and written in Scripture, are not to be expected between the passing of the apostles and the return of Christ (cf. also Heb. 2:2–4). Through the living voice of God the Holy Spirit in Scripture, the same Spirit who indwells all Christians, God continues to reveal himself to us (Eph. 1:13–14, 17–18).

Some day we will know God as perfectly as it is possible for creatures to know him (1 Cor. 13:12).

Note that already we have had to speak about God's nature, about creation, man, sin, Christ, the Spirit, salvation, the church, and the future. A proper understanding of revelation and Scripture cannot be gained apart from a proper understanding of the other major aspects of Christian doctrine.

The importance of a sound understanding of revelation is difficult to exaggerate. If we go looking in the wrong places, or in less than fully reliable places, for the truth about God and his will for us, we are likely to miss the truth. Or, if we go looking in the right place—the Bible—but in the wrong way (denying or minimizing our need of salvation from sin, or denying the trustworthiness of the Bible), we are unlikely to reach the truth. Beyond the matter of personal salvation, a proper understanding of revelation is an indispensable foundation for the Christian life in every aspect, from prayer to evangelism to discernment.

God

There is only one true God, who reveals himself in the Old Testament by the name *Yahweh* or *Jehovah* (Deut. 6:4; Isa. 43:10; 45:5–7; 1 Cor. 8:4–6; 1 Tim. 2:5; James 2:19). He is a totally unique being—no one and nothing is completely like him (1 Kings 8:23; Isa. 40:18, 25; Jer. 10:6–7). As such, he is beyond our comprehension, although we can know him through his self-revelation (Matt. 11:25–27; John 1:18; 1 Cor. 8:2–3).

God is a self-existent spirit, completely distinct from all created things (Isa. 40:22; 43:10; John 4:24; Acts 17:24). At the same time, he is present everywhere and intimately involved in his creation (Ps. 139:7–10; Jer. 23:23–24; Acts 17:27–28). He is eternal and unchangeable (Pss. 90:2, 4; 102:26–27; Mal. 3:6; Eph. 3:21; James 1:17; 2 Pet. 3:8). God is all-powerful—nothing is too hard for him (Gen. 18:14; Jer. 32:17, 27; Matt. 3:9), and all things are possible for him (Job 42:2; Ps. 115:3; Matt. 19:26; Luke 1:37; Eph. 1:11). He knows all things (1 Sam. 16:7; 1 Chron. 28:9, 17; Job 37:16; Ps. 139:1–4; Isa. 41:22–23; 42:9). He is a personal being (Exod. 3:14; Heb. 1:1–2).

God is morally perfect in every way. He is absolutely good (Gen. 1:31; Deut. 8:16; Pss. 107:8; 118:1; Mark 10:18; Rom. 8:28), holy (Lev. 19:2; Pss. 5:4–6; 99:5; Isa. 6:3; Hab. 1:12–13; 1 Pet. 1:14–19), righteous (Isa. 45:21; Zeph. 3:5; Rom. 8:26), and truthful (John 17:17; Titus 1:2; Heb. 6:18). He is perfectly loving (Deut. 7:7–8; Jer. 31:3; John 3:16; Heb. 12:6; 1 John 4:7–8). At the same time, he is righteous in executing judgment against those who reject him (Ps. 103:8–9; Rom. 2:5; 11:22; Heb. 10:31).

It was this incomparable, incomprehensible God who created the world and us (Gen. 1:1; Pss. 33:6; 102:25; Isa. 44:24; John 1:3; Rom. 11:36; Heb. 1:2; 11:3). He is not only our Creator, he is also our Savior (Isa. 43:11; 45:21–22; 1 Tim. 4:10) and the Judge of all mankind (Gen. 18:25; Heb. 12:23; James 4:12).

In the coming of Jesus Christ into the world (John 1:14–18) and then the coming of the Holy Spirit to empower the church (John 14–16), God is revealed to exist in three distinct persons, the Father, Son, and Holy Spirit (Matt. 28:19; Rom. 8:9–11; 1 Cor. 12:4–6; 2 Cor. 13:14; Eph. 2:18; 4:4–6; 1 Pet. 1:2). The Father is God (John 17:3; 1 Cor. 8:6; 2 Cor. 1:3); the Son, Jesus Christ, is God (Isa. 9:6; John 1:1; 20:28; Titus 2:13; Heb. 1:8; 2 Pet. 1:1; 1 John 5:20); and the Holy Spirit is God (Acts 5:3–4; 2 Cor. 3:17–18). These three, while one God, are personally distinct from one another (Matt. 11:27; 28:19; John 3:16–17; 5:31–32; 8:16–18; 14:15–16; 15:26; 16:7, 13–14; 17:23–26; Rom. 8:26–27; 2 John 3).

Once again, the interconnectedness of all Christian doctrine can be seen when the focus is on the doctrine of God. What we think about God is obviously connected with what we think about revelation, Christ, and the Spirit. But we have also seen that our understanding of creation, salvation, the church, and the final judgment is bound up with our view of God.

The heart and essence of Christian doctrine is what it says about God, what it says about the Father, Son, and Holy Spirit. If our God is too small—if we think of God as less than absolutely perfect, as lacking in knowledge, power, presence, or moral excellence—then we will not have absolute, implicit trust in him. If we think of the Son or the Holy Spirit as less than God, then we will fail to give them the honor each is due as fully and truly God. Nothing could be more important than what we think about God.

Christ

Jesus Christ is what Christianity is all about. The entire Old Testament pointed forward to him (Luke 24:25–27, 44). The entire New Testament is God's inspired "commentary" on God's climactic revelation in history, his Son (Heb. 1:1–2). Thus the entire Bible centers on Jesus Christ and what he has done for our salvation.

Jesus Christ is the Son of God; he came into this world as a human being to reveal the Father and to reconcile us to him (John 1:14–18; 3:16; Rom. 5:1–10). He is the eternal God (John 1:1) and the Creator (John 1:3; Col. 1:16). Yet for our sakes and for the Father's glory he humbled himself by taking human form (Phil. 2:6–8). He is therefore both divine and human, both God and man. He was conceived as a man in the womb of Mary through the agency of the Holy Spirit (Matt. 1:18–25; Luke 1:35). He lived a sinless life although subject to human temptations (John 5:19; Heb. 2:18; 4:15). He died a real, agonizing death on the cross, and rose bodily from the grave (Rom. 5:6–10; 1 Cor. 15:3–4). He ascended into heaven, retaining his glorified human form, and will return as such to judge all humanity (Acts 1:9–11; 10:42; 17:31; Col. 2:9; 1

Tim. 2:5). He sent the Holy Spirit to form and empower the church (John 14–16; Acts 1:8). He is deserving of the same honor, love, faith, and worship as God (Matt. 10:37; John 5:23; 14:1; Heb. 1:6).

By now no comment needs to be made about the way all Christian doctrines connect with the doctrine of Christ. This points up the fact that those who ask why we can't simply "believe in Jesus" and not bother about doctrines have missed something. What we think about God, man, sin, the Spirit, salvation, and the future will affect how we think about Christ.

Likewise, the importance of these doctrinal truths about Christ is that they express what Christ really means to the Christian. We are not able to comprehend how Christ can be both God and man; but we can understand that it makes a very big difference whether we believe it or not. If we think of him as less than God, then we won't respond to him with the unconditional love, honor, and trust that he rightfully demands. If we deny his humanity, we effectively deny that he did any of the things the Bible says he did for our salvation—especially his dying a real human death for our sins.

Salvation

The human race is in desperate need of salvation. The enemy from which we need to be saved is ourselves. All of humanity is fallen in sin with our first parent, Adam (Gen. 2:16–17; 3:1–24; Rom. 5:12–21; 1 Cor. 15:22). The result is that we are all sinners, enslaved to sin; none of us is good (Rom. 3:9–23; 7:14–15, 18). As such, we are dead spiritually and deserve nothing but God's righteous wrath (Rom. 6:23; Eph. 2:1–3). This is because the standard by which we are judged is nothing less than the absolute holiness, the perfect moral character, of God (Lev. 19:2). What is true of us individually also holds true corporately. Human institutions, be they families, schools, businesses, religions, nations, governments, societies, civilizations, cultures—all of them, in and of themselves, are corrupted by sin and stand under God's judgment.

In such a condition, there is nothing we can do to contribute to our own salvation. Slaves cannot free themselves; dead men cannot raise themselves. It is not that we are willing to do right but are being prevented; it is rather that we are not willing to do right (Rom. 8:6–8). The darkness of our minds is a self-imposed one (Rom. 1:21–22; Eph. 4:17–19). Trying to be good by our own power, or pursuing our own righteousness, is not the answer (Rom. 9:30–10:3). Our best efforts fall woefully short (Isa. 64:6). Our hearts are so deceitful and wicked that we constantly underestimate the power of sin (Jer. 17:9).

Into our desperate situation God has acted decisively to save us. For our knowledge of God's saving acts and their significance we are completely dependent upon the revelation in Scripture. Beginning with Abraham, God has called to himself a people with whom he established his covenant and to whom he offered salvation individually and corporately (Gen. 12:1–3; 17:1–21; Exod. 19:5–6). The sacrificial, ceremonial system of the covenant God made with Israel anticipated and foreshadowed the sacrificial death of Jesus on the cross for our sins; it has therefore been set aside as having been fulfilled in Christ (Heb. 7:11–10:18). In the new covenant the moral demands of the Old Testament law are fulfilled by the obedience of Christ, and Christians are empowered by the indwelling Spirit of Christ to obey those moral standards from the heart (Rom. 5:19–21; 8:1–11; 13:8–10; Heb. 5:8–9; 1 John 3:4–10).

By his death, Jesus Christ has provided a righteous basis for God to forgive us of our sins and to declare us righteous in his sight (Rom. 3:25–26; 1 John 1:7, 9). This right standing before God is entirely a free gift of God; it cannot be earned, merited, or deserved by us in any way (Rom. 3:24; Eph. 2:8–9; Titus 3:4–7). Nor do we maintain this right standing by good works; rather, good works are the fruit of salvation, performed in the context of a relationship sustained only by God's grace (Eph. 2:10; Titus 3:8). God saves individuals solely through leading them by his grace to repent of their sins and put their faith in Jesus Christ (John 1:12; 3:16–18; Acts 2:38; 17:30–31; Rom. 3:19–28; 4:1–8; 5:1–2; Gal. 2:20). Likewise their progress in living out God's will, their sanctification, is accomplished by God's gracious working through their faith (Rom. 1:17; Gal. 5:6).

The calling of God to salvation is at the same time a call to become members of Christ's body, the church. Entrance into the covenant community of believers in Jesus Christ is through the administration of baptism in water (Matt. 28:19; Acts 2:38; 1 Cor. 12:13). Although the church has a unique status as the redemptive community, God's salvation affects all human institutions, especially families (1 Cor. 7:14; Eph. 5:22–6:4), when those participating in them seek to obey Christ as Lord in their activities (Matt. 28:19–20; Col. 3:17).

Although the basis of salvation is the accomplished work of Christ in dying and rising from the dead, its full realization and consummation are yet future. By God's grace believers will persevere to the end of their lives in faith, and through their faith eventually receive the consummation of their salvation (1 Pet. 1:3–9). The corporate dimensions of salvation, although not completely absent now, will likewise not receive their full realization until the end of history (Rev. 21–22).

Humanity's need and God's provision of salvation are the most fundamental reasons for Christian doctrine. The whole point of doctrine is to safeguard the integrity and faithfulness to the truth of the Christian experience of God's redemptive work. As the preceding summary illustrates, the doctrine of salvation incorporates aspects of all other Christian doctrine. We cannot faithfully preach the good news of salvation unless at the same time we are faithful to the whole doctrinal teaching of Scripture about God, Christ, the church, and the future.

The Church

The church is a people formed by the one, true, living God into a saving relationship with him through his Son, Jesus Christ. Its charter and standard is the revelation of God in Scripture. Its purpose is to love, honor, worship, and obey the triune God, and to reflect his character in the actions of its people. Its basis for existence is the salvation accomplished by Christ and administered or applied to them by the Holy Spirit. Its future is eternal glory in the presence of God.

This church is classically described in the Apostles' *(Nicene!)* Creed as one, holy, catholic, and apostolic. As *one*, the church is a historical, organic unity (1 Cor. 12:12–13; Eph. 2:14–16; 4:4–6, 13–16). It was founded by Christ in the first century, and Christ will return for the same church at his second coming. The church has and will continue to suffer divisions, apostasies, heresies, and scandals, and in some cases what were true churches have become no churches at all (Acts 20:28–30; Rom. 16:17; 1 Cor. 11:18–19; 2 Cor. 11:4, 13–15; Gal. 1:6–8; 1 Tim. 4:1; Titus 3:10–11; 1 John 2:19; Jude 17–19; Rev. 2–3). However, there will always be a true church worshiping the true God and keeping, although imperfectly, the true faith, until Christ's return (Matt. 16:18; 28:18–20; Eph. 3:21; 4:11–16; Jude 4).

This church is *holy*, then, not in the sense that it is perfect or even admirable in character, but in the sense that it has been consecrated to God and is therefore a unique institution through which God is working to accomplish his redemptive purpose in history. As such those who identify themselves as its members individually have the promise of all spiritual blessings in Christ if they believe (Eph. 1:3–14) and God's most severe judgment if they disbelieve (Heb. 2:1–3; 4:1–2; 10:29–31).

The church is also described as *catholic*. As I explained in chapter 6, the Greek word *katholikos* means "universal," and does not refer distinctly to the Roman Catholic

Church. The true church includes the association of all true believers in Jesus Christ throughout the world and throughout history. This is really nothing more than another way of stating that the church is one.

Here I would like to offer an observation which, strictly speaking, goes beyond the issue of orthodox doctrine. The doctrine of catholicity cuts in two ways. On the one hand, since the true church includes all Christian churches, no denominational institution or association of churches today can claim exclusively to be the only true church. This is a claim traditionally made by both the Roman Catholic and Eastern Orthodox churches. Although these churches have always qualified their claim to admit the existence of Christians outside their walls, the claim is still at odds with a biblical concept of catholicity. On the other hand, the Roman and Eastern churches are right in their insistence that the church's oneness *ought* to be reflected institutionally. Protestants, in their zeal to defend the integrity of their churches, have often tried to deny this. Denominational divisions are symptomatic of sin in the church. We may disagree as to where the fault lies, but we ought to be able to admit this much. Making the local congregation completely autonomous and eschewing all denominations does not solve this problem, either; all that results is that each congregation becomes its own denomination. My point is not that we should abandon all denominational divisions tomorrow, but that we should work to overcome unnecessary divisions in the church.

Finally, the church is *apostolic*. This has been held to mean one of two things. In the view of Roman Catholics, Eastern Orthodox, and Anglicans (Episcopalians), it means that the church was established as an institution with the apostles commissioning bishops, who in turn commissioned the next generation of bishops, and so on down through the centuries. In this view, only churches that have bishops who can trace their ordination back to the apostles are part of the "apostolic" church. This doctrine is commonly called apostolic succession, although of course bishops are not regarded as apostles. In the view of Protestants, the church is apostolic if it upholds the doctrine of the apostles as preserved in Scripture. This means that churches with bishops are apostolic only if they adhere to the doctrine of the apostles (some have not), while churches without bishops are apostolic if they adhere to apostolic doctrine (some do, some don't).

It is not within my purpose here to argue this matter out. Obviously, the position I have taken as to the meaning of catholicity commits me to the Protestant view. However, I do not see the apostolic succession view as all wrong. In keeping with the doctrine of the unity of the church, I would agree that there must be some historical linkage between modern-day churches and the apostles. There must be some continuity by which the same faith is transmitted from one generation to the next. Any specific church or denomination must be able to show that its faith has its roots in the church's historical development from the apostles to the present. One may (and must, if he or she is a Protestant) maintain that this development has at times necessitated reformation, confrontation of church officials, and even separation from those segments of the church that have abandoned the faith for liberalism or other apostate doctrines. But no group can turn its back on the church, abandon the faith upheld by the church throughout the centuries, and seek to be "apostolic" by adopting a novel reinterpretation of the apostles' teaching in the New Testament. Such groups are not apostolic, because to be apostolic means not only to uphold apostolic doctrine but also to be part of the church founded by the apostles. This, as I see it, is the truth in the non-Protestant understanding of apostolicity. The difference is that I maintain, along with Protestants generally, that this historical apostolicity need not be tied exclusively to a succession of bishops.

As the above treatment illustrates, the doctrine of the church is an area of much greater disagreement among

Christians than perhaps any other. Yet its importance for orthodoxy and for doctrinal discernment is very great. Wrong views of the church can, in the worst cases, keep people from salvation. Some people think so little of the church that they imagine they can safely abandon the historic faith of the church and reinvent Christianity. Others think so highly of the church that they imagine that mere membership in its ranks or participation in its activities will save them. Both errors are fatal spiritually. Less extreme errors may not keep people from being saved, but they can keep them from experiencing a full, robust Christian life by separating them from whole segments of the church.

The Future

The much-talked about differences among orthodox Christians regarding the future, or "end-times," should not be allowed to obscure the substantial agreements that exist on the essentials. History is being moved by God toward a time of consummation, a time when all of God's purposes in creating and redeeming the human race will be fulfilled (Rev. 21–22). When this goal is reached, the partial understanding that we have of God's revelation of himself in the historic incarnate Christ and in Scripture will give way to a full, perfect (for creatures) understanding as we come face to face with God in Christ (1 Cor. 13:9–12; 1 John 3:1–2).

When this consummation is reached, God's rule over all creation will be uncontested. All creatures enjoying God's world will know, love, and obey God perfectly and joyfully (Isa. 11:9; Zech. 14:9; Mark 12:28–34; Eph. 1:11). The character of God will be perfectly imaged by human beings individually and corporately (Eph. 4:24; Col. 3:10). The new human race, redeemed and perfected, will be conformed perfectly to the image of Jesus Christ (Rom. 8:29; 1 Cor. 15:48–49; Phil. 3:21). Their salvation, accomplished with certainty by Christ in his death and resurrection and secured for them individually by the sealing of the indwelling Holy Spirit, will be brought to consummation in the redemption of their bodies and the glorification of their entire beings with immortal, heavenly, Spirit-empowered life (Rom. 8:18–30; 1 Cor. 15:42–54; 2 Cor. 5:1–5; Eph. 1:13–14; Col. 3:1–4). The result will be a glorious society of perfect creatures fit for life in the new heavens and new earth, in which only righteousness will dwell (2 Pet. 3:13; Rev. 21:1).

Entrance into this glorious eternity is not guaranteed for all. Both fallen angels and all human beings (except Jesus Christ) deserve eternal punishment; and those whom God does not save through Jesus Christ will suffer such eternal punishment (Matt. 25:46; 2 Thess. 1:7–9; Rev. 20:10–15).

What will occur between now and the consummation is of greatest controversy among Christians. What we know is that the timing of Christ's return is not revealed to us. It will come upon all suddenly and without warning. It will catch unbelievers unaware because they do not expect him to come at all, while it will bring joy and relief to believers who did not know when to expect him but were faithfully doing his will knowing that he would return (Matt. 24:36–51; 1 Thess. 5:1–11).

The meaning of the Millennium (Rev. 20:1–6) is hotly disputed among orthodox Christians. Yet what all agree is that it refers to a period—whether present or future, before or after the second coming of Christ—that precedes the final consummation. It is therefore a reminder to us that Christ's rule in human hearts and over human institutions can never be complete until sin is completely removed by Christ's final judgment, bringing eternal punishment on the unbelieving and sifting the works of believers in preparation for their eternal life in God's new world (Rom. 14:10–12; 1 Cor. 3:12–15; 2 Cor. 5:10).

The significance and importance of the doctrine of God's purposes for the future should not be missed. We do not know exactly what things will be like in the eternal state God has planned for us (1 John 3:2). But we are not completely ignorant of where we are going. If we disagree radically on where we are going, we are not going to be agreed on how to get there. The biblical doctrine of the future makes clear once again that salvation is a work of God's grace in Jesus Christ. We are totally helpless to bring about the consummation. Yet by God's grace he works through us to move history closer to that goal (2 Pet. 3:11–12). The study of sound doctrine is one means by which we can grow in the grace and knowledge of our Lord Jesus Christ, to whom we give glory now and will do so in eternity (2 Pet. 3:18). And that is the whole point of sound doctrine.

11

Who Should Judge?

How shall the identification of heresy be carried out in practice? Specifically, who shall be involved in the process of identifying and responding to heresy? And in what way shall they be involved? Here I wish simply to give some brief suggestions as guidelines that seem to me to be in keeping with the teaching of Scripture.

I have already argued in chapters 3 and 4 that the Christian church as a whole is responsible for exercising discernment or judgment concerning heretical teachings, and that such judgment should not be left solely in the hands of trusted religious leaders, no matter who they are. Here I wish to sharpen this point somewhat.

Ultimately, only God can judge human hearts, since only he knows infallibly what people are thinking and feeling. We do not even know our own hearts infallibly (Jer. 17:9–10). Therefore, when we speak about judging heresy, we are not claiming to know the hearts of those espousing the heresy. We are not setting ourselves up as arbiters of their eternal future, deciding who will be saved and who will not.

What the church is called to judge is whether certain teachings should be allowed to be propagated in its midst, whether certain practices should be condoned, and whether certain individuals espousing heretical teachings or immoral practices should be allowed to remain in the community of faith. This kind of judgment is to be exercised by the whole church, although some persons in the church will play a more direct role in the process than others.

There are commands in the New Testament directing all Christians to exercise discernment (1 Cor. 5:9–13; 14:29; 1 John 4:1). Yet, some Christians are more gifted or skilled in such discernment than others. God gives some Christians special gifts of discernment concerning spirits (1 Cor. 12:10). God gives some Christians gifts enabling them to be teachers (Rom. 12:6–7; 1 Cor. 12:28–29; Eph. 4:11; James 3:1). God has also called some Christians to be in positions of leadership in the church—such as pastors, elders, overseers, deacons—and they will clearly have a more direct role in carrying out the judgment of the church concerning heresy (Acts 20:28; Phil. 1:1; Eph. 4:11; 1 Tim. 3:1–13; Titus 1:5–9; Heb. 13:17; 1 Pet. 5:1–3). For this reason, such Christian leaders should inform themselves and consult with gifted Christian teachers to make sure that mature discernment is exercised in their congregation. And the leaders and teachers should work together to instruct the church body as a whole in sound doctrine and in the practice of discernment, so that the whole body will indeed be of one mind in its discernment.

The Role of Church Bodies

Although all Christians are called to be discerning and to take responsibility for the doctrine they believe and pass on to others, not all Christians are called to discipline false teachers. This is the sole responsibility of church bodies. All churches have (or at least they should have) some structure or procedure for handling false teachers. Typically, it begins at the congregational level. An individual congregation may have a problem with a teacher in the church who is espousing false doctrine. That congregation is responsible to prevent the false teacher from continuing to teach there. In many cases a higher level of church authority is brought into the matter, whether that higher level is a bishop or superintendent or presbytery or whatever.

I am unconcerned here with the ecclesiastical structure in which these matters are resolved. Different denominations utilize different structures, and even if one is better than the others, all church bodies are responsible to exercise discipline in doctrinal matters. And that is the point I wish to emphasize here. Every church body is responsible for maintaining doctrinal faithfulness to orthodoxy. Moreover, it is only church bodies that can excommunicate heretics. All Christians are called to exercise discernment, but only church bodies are called to exercise church discipline.

The Role of Parachurch Ministries

If only church bodies can exercise church discipline, then what role should parachurch ministries play? This is an especially acute question to ask today, since there are now hundreds of parachurch discernment and countercult ministries throughout the world publicly criticizing false teachers both inside and outside the institutional Christian church. Is there any place for such ministries?

The answer is yes, there is a place for such ministries, but it is a limited one. Parachurch discernment ministries can legitimately exist to *instruct Christians* and to *advise church bodies*. Remember that all Christians have the responsibility to exercise discernment, but only church bodies have the responsibility to exercise discipline. Parachurch ministries can serve all Christians in educating them in doctrinal discernment. They can teach them sound doctrine, warn them about false doctrine, and provide information about organizations, teachers, and publications promoting false doctrine. What Christians as individuals do with such instruction and information, however, is not for parachurch ministries to decide. They can instruct but not command.

Likewise, parachurch ministries can serve church bodies by advising them in their responsibility of church discipline. They can provide information, offer guidelines and insight, and even assist church bodies in their investigation into doctrinal controversies. What church bodies conclude and what they do, however, is not for parachurch ministries to decide. They can advise but not dictate.

Parachurch ministries, then, are not official arbiters of orthodoxy and heresy. They are free to express their evaluations and judgments publicly after following proper procedures, but those evaluations and judgments are, from a churchly perspective, nonbinding. Of course, if those judgments are true, then churches ought to bind themselves by them—but not merely because some parachurch organization says so.

Within these limitations, parachurch discernment ministries can serve the body of Christ in invaluable ways. Because they tend to be highly specialized, they can provide expert guidance in understanding sometimes difficult questions. Parachurch ministries are able to reach many people who have not been effectively reached through traditional church evangelism. Parachurch ministries, because they are not officially tied to one denomination or church, can often bring a greater objectivity to doctrinal controversies within a particular church body. For these and other reasons, parachurch ministries that specialize in doctrinal discernment can be and are of immense importance.

The "Ten Commandments" of Discernment

t last we come to the "nitty-gritty" of discernment. Just what should we do in order to exercise sound doctrinal discernment? How should we go about becoming more mature and skilled in discernment? The following "ten commandments" are not exhaustive, but they are especially critical.

(1) *Learn to exercise discernment while growing as a Christian in faith, love, and holiness.* I would like to assume this is obvious to everyone, but it bears emphasizing and even placing first on the list. The Christian life is not an intellectual game in which the object is to prove that you are right and to ferret out everyone who is wrong. Discerning orthodox from heretical teaching is only one aspect of the Christian life, although it is an important one. Moreover, doctrinal discernment itself should involve prayer, fellowship with other Christians, ministry to other Christians and to the lost, and doctrinal study. May I also say that I am preaching to myself here

more than to anyone else! As one whose lifetime ministry and career is concentrated in the practice and communication of doctrinal discernment, I (and my colleagues in discernment ministry, as well) am more apt to forget this than other Christians.

On the other hand, let me also emphasize the word *growing* in the above statement. There is not some minimum standard of spiritual achievement that must be reached before one may begin exercising discernment. Rather, the exercise of discernment is one function in the Christian life in which all believers should be growing throughout their Christian experience.

(2) *Develop a thorough and sound grasp of Scripture.* Other things being equal, the better one understands the Bible, the better one will be able to discern truth from error. Not every Christian can be a Bible scholar, but virtually every Christian can study the Bible in depth and gain a profound understanding of its teachings.

There are various ways in which one can study the Bible, and all of them are important. Read the Bible itself—read whole books of the Bible, and read the whole Bible (although not necessarily in any particular order). Commit portions of Scripture to memory. Study the Bible topically, searching through Scripture and reading what it says on particular subjects (see Acts 17:11). Use study aids, theological textbooks, and the like (although discernment will be needed in choosing and using such works). Study the Bible by yourself and in groups. Find competent teachers and learn as much as you can from them. The point is to use every resource possible to increase your understanding of Scripture.

(3) *Learn to think in a logical, sensitive manner.* Logic and sensitivity sound like opposites to some people, but they are not. To think logically means to think in such a way as to avoid drawing false conclusions from true premises. The whole purpose of the study of logic is to master the art of thinking clearly. It is possible to have all

the facts and reach a false conclusion, if the way one interprets those facts is faulty.

Unfortunately, some people zealous for logical thinking sometimes apply logical analysis in an insensitive manner. By this I do not mean that they are rude or uncaring (this might or might not be the case). Rather, I mean that they draw seemingly logical conclusions without full appreciation for the complexities or nuances of the situation. Their thinking is logical in a sort of flat-footed way. The usual result is that the errors of a particular religious teacher or group are exaggerated or even misidentified.

In short, thinking that is lacking in sensitivity, as I am using that term, is thinking that is in actuality illogical. A conclusion is drawn without considering all of the facts— a logical error usually called a hasty generalization or hasty conclusion. Or a conclusion is drawn about someone's beliefs without full appreciation of the distinctive ways that the person uses terminology. Making that mistake in logic is called equivocating—drawing a conclusion from premises that use the same word but in two different senses.

Poor reasoning is a major problem in the field of doctrinal discernment today. We all need to refine and improve our reasoning ability to the fullest extent we can as we seek to be discerning in doctrinal matters.

(4) _Study Christian doctrine from a variety of traditions within orthodox Christianity._ As you become fairly clear on the essentials of the faith, you should seek to become familiar with some of the different perspectives on Christian doctrine within the household of faith. You will want to acquaint yourself with different views held by Christians on such controversial doctrinal matters as baptism, the Millennium, spiritual gifts, predestination, and the like. Understanding the different perspectives held by orthodox Christians on these doctrinal matters will enable you to appreciate better the difference between essentials and nonessentials of the faith, as well as to gain a more mature and biblical position on them.

Good

(5) *Learn as much relevant information as possible about a questionable teaching or religious group before making any judgment.* Scripture says, "He who gives an answer before he hears, it is folly and shame to him" (Prov. 18:13). It is sin for Christians to judge someone's beliefs as heretical on the basis of less than adequate information.

There are a variety of strategies you can use to gain information about a group. You can inquire about religious affiliations—the denomination or religion of a teacher or group—although in some cases certain organizations or persons may deny their controversial religious affiliations. You can ask for information about their history or leaders, as sometimes this is illuminating. You can consult standard reference works, dictionaries, or encyclopedias that list religious groups and organizations and describe their beliefs. In most cases, except with very new or small groups or teachings, these strategies will give you adequate information.

(6) *Base your understanding of a questionable doctrine on what those who espouse it say about it themselves, but do not assume that the use of orthodox language guarantees orthodox beliefs.* Just as we would not want someone to label us heretics or accuse us of other evils (Matt. 5:11) on the basis of what others say about us, so we should not criticize others' views without being sure that we have heard them firsthand (Matt. 7:12). This does not mean that every Christian must personally read the primary literature of a heretical group before concluding that it is indeed heretical. Rather, a Christian critique of a supposedly heretical group should be considered less than adequate to the extent that the accusations made are not backed up with accurate quotations from the authoritative leaders of the group.

In questionable cases where no adequate Christian analysis or evaluation has yet been done, it is very important to gain primary source information about the group's doctrines. One approach that is often helpful is to ask for a doctrinal statement. However, keep in mind the following two observations: First, some groups that have no doctrinal statement are nevertheless orthodox. Second, doctrinal statements of heretical groups are often kept as orthodox-sounding as possible to avoid easy criticism. Other publications may be more revealing of the group's true colors.

It is, in fact, a mark of unorthodox and aberrant groups that they are often not straightforward and honest about the true nature of their beliefs. They will frequently use biblical language and sound very evangelical in order to avoid criticism. This is exactly what the New Testament warns us about (e.g., 2 Cor. 11:4).

In the case of groups that are dishonest about their true beliefs, gather as much information about their beliefs as possible and compare what they say *to the public* with what they say *to one another*. This may involve attending their meetings and asking questions without seeming critical (see Matt. 10:16) or obtaining in-house literature normally available only to members. Generally, such investigations should be carried out by those with some experience and training in doctrinal discernment, such as those involved in discernment ministries. In some cases, ex-members may be the best source of such information and materials.

(7) *Treat the information supplied by ex-members with both respect and due caution.* Every heretical group eventually begins generating ex-members in greater or lesser quantities, and these persons can be invaluable resources. Often their most important contribution is their access to publications and recordings unavailable to the general public. Their personal testimonies can also be very informative and helpful.

One of the marks of a heretical or aberrant group is that its ex-members are all dismissed as disgruntled or envious or immoral persons with an axe to grind. Of course, this may be true of some ex-members. Yet, if a religious group loses a large number of people, and these ex-members consistently tell the same story, their testimony should be given due credence. If an ex-member can back up his (or her) story with documentation or corroborative testimony from other ex-members, that will serve to reinforce his testimony.

Occasionally, certain individuals will present themselves as ex-members of a group and tell sensational stories about their involvement. Great caution must be exercised in such cases, as increasingly there are instances of persons doing this who either were never part of the group in question, or were never as deeply involved as they claim. Whether such individuals perpetuate such deceptions for financial gain, media attention, personal antagonism toward the group, or for more subtle reasons, may not always be clear. In any case it is important that sensationalistic accusations against a group not be accepted on the basis of the testimony of one person or couple apart from corroborative evidence.

(8) *In uncertain or borderline cases, give the benefit of the doubt to the person or group in question.* The principle of "innocent until proven guilty" applies here. Some Christians involved in discernment ministries raise "red flags" or, to change the metaphor, "cry wolf" whenever there is the slightest hint of possible heresy. Such a practice brings reproach upon discernment ministries and divides Christians.

(9) *Begin with foundational matters.* In inquiring into the orthodoxy of a religious group, much time and energy can be saved and mistakes prevented by asking foundational questions about the group's attitude toward the Bible and religious authority. Do they regard the Bible as the absolutely infallible, unerring Word of God? Do they regard the Bible as the final authority in religious matters, or do they look to something else (their leaders, a modern prophet, another book, etc.) as an indispensable authority by which the Bible is interpreted? If their answers to these questions are satisfactory, then in most cases they will be orthodox; if not, they will usually be

heretical. Keep in mind that some heretical groups profess complete confidence in the Bible and appear to have no other doctrinal authorities; thus, this guideline should be treated only as a rule of thumb.

(10) *Consult with reputable discernment ministries that honor biblical principles of discernment.* No human being is infallible, nor is any organization, including Christian discernment ministries. Nevertheless, if you agree that the principles discussed in this book are biblical, then you should consult with discernment ministries who seek to base their work on these principles. (Recall what was said in the previous chapter about such parachurch discernment ministries.) A list of recommended discernment organizations is provided at the end of this book.

The Challenge of Discernment

In conclusion, I would like to offer a challenge to those who agree that doctrinal discernment of the kind discussed in this book is necessary. Begin to do something to contribute to the ongoing task of discernment. Encourage your church leaders to preach and teach on doctrinal discernment. Support one or more biblically based discernment ministries, especially any that may be in your local area. If you are a parent, teach sound doctrine to your children. Pray for sound Christian teachers and preachers, and pray that heresies and aberrant doctrines would lose their appeal. Every Christian can and should be doing something to contribute to the church's discernment of sound doctrine.

APPENDIX A

Checking Out
a Church's Teaching

Y ou, or someone you know, is looking into becoming part of a particular church. How do you go about checking out the church's teaching? In addition to the general recommendations made in the last chapter of this book, I would like to offer some guidelines for checking into a specific church's teaching.

(1) *Have a clear idea what kind of teaching you want.* This sounds obvious once it is said. First of all, hopefully, you are committed to orthodox teaching. But there are degrees of sound doctrine even among orthodox churches. There are two sorts of questions you might ask.

First, you can ask, does this church take doctrine seriously in a balanced way? You want a church that gives its people both doctrinal "milk" (teaching for new and immature believers) and "meat" (teaching for those pressing on to maturity in their faith). Some churches seem to offer nothing but Sunday school classes on family, money, and other doctrinally "lightweight" topics; other churches seem to ignore these highly practical, down-to-earth topics. So, you want a balance. You also want a church that is teaching sound doctrine on a broad range of doctrinal issues. Some churches, unfortunately, seem to teach on only one doctrinal subject (be it justification by faith, spiritual gifts, or the end-times). Again, a balance is needed. But remember that no church can be teaching on everything all the time!

Second, you can ask, does this church take any doctrinal stand that I will have a hard time supporting? Another way to ask the question is this: If I brought someone to this church and they heard this teaching, would I be embarrassed? You will have to decide which doctrines these will be. On some issues you ought to be able to be flexible, because they are not crucial; but on others, you may decide that you need to take a stand. This question will often be more important to someone who expects to be involved in the church's teaching ministry. After all, it's one thing to attend a church that teaches a different view of the Millennium than you personally believe; it's another thing to be asked to teach that different view yourself.

(2) *Inquire about religious affiliations.* A church's name may or may not tell you much about its beliefs. The first step in such cases is to ask whether it is a part of a denomination or association of churches, and which one.

(3) *Ask for a doctrinal statement.* Many churches have their own doctrinal statement, even those that are part of a denomination. Be discerning as you read the statement. Some doctrinal statements on certain subjects express details that go beyond what they expect every member to accept, although their teachers all abide by them. This is often true on such subjects as infant baptism, the Millennium, and spiritual gifts. Other doctrinal statements do not tell you enough, or are deliberately vague so as to be as inoffensive as possible to those with concerns for doctrinal purity. Yet other churches profess to subscribe to historic creeds or confessions, but ignore them or reinterpret them on the basis of a liberal theology. So be discerning.

(4) *Find out who founded the church or denomination, and who its leaders are today.* Sometimes you may be stuck to identify what a church really stands for until you discover who its founder or present-day leader is.

(5) *Consult standard reference works.* Several encyclopedic reference works exist that contain significant information on most of the religious groups you are likely to encounter. Of course, very small and new groups will not be mentioned. The following are some of the best:

Evangelical Dictionary of Theology, edited by Walter A. Elwell (Grand Rapids: Baker, 1984). Medium-length articles on major theological movements, issues, and theologians.

The New International Dictionary of the Christian Church, edited by J. D. Douglas (Grand Rapids: Zondervan, 1978). Typically short articles on specific individuals, events, sects, denominations, and groups.

The Encyclopedia of American Religions, by J. Gordon Melton, 2d ed. (Detroit: Gale Research, 1987). The most exhaustive work of its kind, listing practically every religious group of whatever kind in America (and most elsewhere, too) with more than a few hundred members (and many smaller ones as well). Not written from an evangelical perspective, but generally accurate and helpful.

Appendix B

On Using the Word *Cult*

What do you think of when you hear the word *cult*? Chances are that you think of an oppressive religious group with a dictatorial leadership that practices a severe form of mind control over its members. Such cults do exist, of course, and they are of concern to everyone, including non-Christians.

However, evangelical Protestants tend to use the word *cult* to refer to both such socially and psychologically destructive groups and other groups that may be more socially acceptable. Often evangelicals call a group a cult if it espouses heresy, regardless of its social character. Obviously, this can be confusing to people, and unnecessarily offensive to members of such theological "cults."

My recommendation is that Christians avoiding labeling groups as cults unless they fit the usual sociological and psychological profile of a cult as understood even by non-Christians. Of course, if such a group also espouses heresy, it will be a cult in that theological sense as well. But in my judgment the time has come to admit that using the word *cult* to refer to socially mainstream religious groups that espouse heresy is counterproductive.

When referring to heretical religious groups, I prefer to call them heretical religions, or pseudo-Christian religions, or heretical sects. These labels are more descriptive and less prejudicial than the label of cult. Of course, no one likes being called a heretic or pseudo-Christian. But you stand a better chance of being understood using these expressions than if you call them a cult.

By no means do I advocate backing off calling a group a cult if they deserve the label. Some religions are cults in the most sinister sense possible. But you will rarely gain a hearing if you call someone's religion a cult to their face. They are likely to think that they cannot be a cult because they know very well that they are normal people who joined their religion freely, who love their families, and who live responsible lives in their communities.

For that matter, it does little good to use labels at all when confronting people in false religious systems. It is better to be as descriptive and nonabrasive in your language as possible. But if you are asked for your assessment of a group, you should not hesitate to call it cultic or heretical or apostate if the shoe fits. The principle to follow in all such situations is to speak the truth in love (Eph. 4:15).

Glossary

aberrational—Off-center or in error in some important way, such that the doctrine or practice should be rejected and those who accept it held to be sinning, even though they may very well be Christian. Also called **aberrant**. See chapter 6.

apostasy—A falling away or departure from a previously maintained orthodox position (as in certain denominations which once held to orthodoxy but have rejected it). Adj.: **apostate**.

biblical—Agreeing with or faithful to the teaching of the Bible. Whatever is contrary to its teaching is **unbiblical**, although this word is usually used only when the biblical teaching violated is clear and of signal importance.

cult—(1) A religious group originating as a heretical sect and maintaining fervent commitment to heresy. (2) A religious or semireligious group which exhibits extreme antisocial behavior. Adj.: **cultic**, which may be used with reference to tendencies as well as full cult status. See Appendix B.

denomination—A religious body originating as a Christian movement or sect and generally classified as a Christian body regardless of its doctrinal orthodoxy.

discern—To identify the true nature of a spirit, doctrine, practice, or group; to distinguish truth from error,

115

extreme error from slight error, the divine from the human and the demonic.

doctrine—Content of teaching intended to be accepted and believed as truth.

dogma—Doctrine which a church or sect expects all its members to accept in order to remain in good standing; or, one which a church or sect expects its members to accept simply on the church's or sect's authority. Adj.: **dogmatic**.

excommunication—A church disciplinary action in which a person who refuses to repent of promoting heretical views, or of engaging in gross sin, is no longer accepted as a member of the church. Such a person may not participate in the ordinances of the church, may not teach or minister in any way, and in extreme cases may be asked to refrain from attending church meetings. Sometimes called **disfellowshiping**.

heresy—Doctrine which is erroneous in such a way that Christians must divide themselves as a church from all who teach or accept it; those adhering to heresy are assumed to be lost, although Christians are unable to make definitive judgments on this matter. The opposite of orthodoxy. Adj.: **heretical**. See chapter 5.

heterodox—Differing from orthodox teaching in some significant way; may occur in varying degrees.

orthodoxy—The body of essential biblical teachings. Those who embrace them should be accepted as Christians. The opposite of heresy. Adj.: **orthodox**. See chapter 5.

orthopraxis—Correct practice required of anyone who would be regarded as a Christian.

schism—A division within a religious group, especially one which divides Christians from one another. Adj.: **schismatic**.

sect—A religious group formed as the result of schism, especially one which is fairly small and of relatively recent origin. Adj.: **sectarian**.

sound—Agreeing with and faithful to biblical teaching and to orthodoxy beyond a bare minimum, such that Christians may be encouraged to continue in this way. Contrasted with aberrational, which refers to teaching or practice which is only barely or inconsistently orthodox. Its opposite, **unsound**, may be used to express degrees of deficiency in soundness.

suborthodox—Less than orthodox, yet not explicitly contrary to orthodoxy.

unorthodox—Departing from orthodoxy in some measure, although not necessarily embracing explicit heresy.

RECOMMENDED READING

Alnor, William M. *Soothsayers of the Second Advent.* Old Tappan, N.J.: Fleming H. Revell, 1989.
An exposé of the "prophetic games" that even Christians play, including date setting, speculations about the identity of the Antichrist, "666 Madness," and other errors.

Bray, Gerald. *Creeds, Councils and Christ.* Leicester, England: Inter-Varsity, 1984.
Historical study which defends the creeds as faithful expressions of biblical teaching.

Brown, Harold O. J. *Heresies: The Image of Christ in the Mirror of Heresy and Orthodoxy from the Apostles to the Present.* Grand Rapids: Baker, 1988.
A survey of church history focusing on orthodox responses to heresy.

Bussell, Harold. *Unholy Devotion: Why Cults Lure Christians.* Grand Rapids: Zondervan, 1983.
Doctrinal and nondoctrinal factors that mislead even Christians, and which lure people into cults. Very easy reading.

Davis, John Jefferson. *Foundations of Evangelical Theology.* Grand Rapids: Baker, 1984.
An excellent textbook discussing the nature of evangelical theology and its view of reason, experience, Scripture, and tradition.

———, ed. *The Necessity of Systematic Theology,* 2d ed. Grand Rapids: Baker, 1978.

119

A collection of essays on the importance of doctrine to the lay Christian.

Erickson, Millard J. *Christian Theology.* 1 vol. ed. Grand Rapids: Baker, 1988.
Currently the best complete evangelical systematic theology textbook.

Frame, John M. *The Doctrine of the Knowledge of God: A Theology of Lordship.* Phillipsburg, N.J.: Presbyterian & Reformed, 1987.
On theological and apologetical method. Has a very helpful discussion on creeds and confessions, an excellent treatment on using logic in a sensitive manner, and much more.

————. *Evangelical Reunion: Denominations and the Body of Christ.* Grand Rapids: Baker, 1991.
Why Christians must work to break down denominational barriers that separate true Christians without compromising sound doctrine, and how we can begin. I wish every Christian would read this book.

Geisler, Norman L., and Ronald M. Brooks. *Come, Let Us Reason: An Introduction to Logical Thinking.* Grand Rapids: Baker, 1990.
The importance of logical thinking for discernment can hardly be overrated; this is the best logic textbook written for Christians, with many illustrations from theology and apologetics.

Miller, Elliot. "The Christian and Authority." *Forward* 8, 1 (Spring 1985):8–15; 8, 2 (Summer 1985):8–11, 24–26.
Argues that the church, reason, and experience are all important but subordinate to Scripture in authority. Reprints available from CRI (see *Discernment Ministries* for information).

————. *A Crash Course on the New Age Movement: Describing and Evaluating a Growing Social Force.* Grand Rapids: Baker, 1989.
A model critique of a non-Christian religious philosophy that avoids sensationalistic or exploitative exaggerations.

Passantino, Robert, and Gretchen Passantino. *Witch Hunt.* Nashville: Thomas Nelson, 1990.

A critique of faulty methods of exercising doctrinal discernment that are often used to label Christian groups mistakenly as heretical or cultic. Contains numerous examples of such faulty reasoning, which the Passantinos label *witch hunting.* Although I do not always agree with the details of their argument, overall I am in solid agreement with the approach taken and the concerns expressed in this book.

Poythress, Vern S. *Symphonic Theology: The Validity of Multiple Perspectives in Theology.* Grand Rapids: Zondervan/Academie, 1987.

Distinguishing substantive disagreement from different but complementary perspectives; much of what I have written about the perspectival nature of doctrine comes from this book.

Discernment Ministries

The following is a short list of Christian ministries that specialize in doctrinal discernment. Ministries that focus on one specific heretical or cultic group are not listed here. For referrals to such ministries, contact CRI, or obtain the *Directory of Cult Research Organizations* by Eric Pement and Keith Edward Tolbert (available from American Religions Center, listed below). The author is associated with CRI.

American Religions Center (ARC)
P.O. Box 168, Trenton, MI 48183
(313) 425-7788

Research organization specializing in computerizing access to information on apologetics and discernment-related issues. Keith E. Tolbert is the president.

Christian Research Institute (CRI)
P.O. Box 500, San Juan Capistrano, CA 92693-0500
(714) 855-9926

Founded by the late Dr. Walter Martin. Hank Hanegraaff is the president. Produces the "Bible Answer Man" radio program heard on numerous stations in the United States and Canada. Publishes a major periodical called the *Christian Research Journal*. Has a branch office in Sao Paulo, Brazil.

Personal Freedom Outreach (PFO)
P.O. Box 26062, St. Louis, MO 63136
(314) 388-2648

A network of discernment ministries with about half a dozen chapters in the United States; publishes a major newsletter called the *PFO Quarterly Journal.* Kurt Goedelman is the director.

Spiritual Counterfeits Project (SCP)
P.O. Box 4308, Berkeley, CA 94704
(415) 540–0300

Disseminates literature with special focus on mystical and occult religious themes. Tal Brooke is the president.

Watchman Fellowship
P.O. Box 7681, Columbus, GA 31908
(404) 576–4321

A network of discernment ministries with about a dozen chapters in the United States. David Hanke is the president.

Scripture Index

125

Subject Index